# OPTIMIZE

## HOW TO ATTRACT AND ENGAGE MORE CUSTOMERS BY INTEGRATING SEO, SOCIAL MEDIA, AND CONTENT MARKETING

## LEE ODDEN

WILEY

John Wiley & Sons, Inc.

Published by John Wiley & Sons, Inc., Hoboken, New Jersey.
Published simultaneously in Canada.

For general information on our other products and services or for technical support, please contact our Customer Care Department within the United States at (800) 762-2974, outside the United States at (317) 572-3993 or fax (317) 572-4002.

Wiley publishes in a variety of print and electronic formats and by print-on-demand. Some material included with standard print versions of this book may not be included in e-books or in print-on-demand. If this book refers to media such as a CD or DVD that is not included in the version you purchased, you may download this material at http://booksupport.wiley.com. For more information about Wiley products, visit www.wiley.com.

ISBN 978-1-118-16777-9 (cloth); ISBN 978-1-118-22638-4 (ebk);
ISBN 978-1-118-23957-5 (ebk); ISBN 978-1-118-26427-0 (ebk)

Printed in the United States of America

10  9  8  7  6  5  4  3  2  1

# Contents

# Foreword

It's time to leave some of the old wisdom behind and develop some new wisdom.
—Mike Grehan being interviewed by Lee Odden in 2007

I keep bumping into Lee Odden. All over the world, in fact. For the past four or five years, at conferences from New York to San Francisco, London to Barcelona, and Hong Kong to Singapore, we've discussed the subject of Internet marketing. These are deeply engaging conversations for one very important reason. When it comes to marketing, Lee Odden gets it.

As a classically trained marketer, Lee cuts through the clutter of the pipes-and-tubes element of Internet marketing to focus on content and customers. Already, he has a huge following on social networking sites such as Twitter, Facebook, and LinkedIn. This is largely due to his steady transition from popular blogger and industry commentator to recognized thought leader.

Inspired by a "lightbulb moment" in conversation with a Google engineer, he was prompted into thinking about Internet marketing and business in new and different ways. It's a new kind of wisdom, partly based on practical experience and partly based on training his mind to see around corners.

We've had an era of search marketing being front and center. But as we move into a new era of the constantly connected consumer with the prediction that, in a few years there'll be 50 billion connected devices on the planet, it really is time to change the way we think about marketing. And this is not being driven purely by technology, it's more about the change in the consumer—the new, transient media consumer.

Much of what we've learned in marketing is undergoing reconsideration. Major changes are taking place in consumer and business markets. Consumers no longer act independently of each other but are more connected to other consumers, to other channel members, and often to brands. Consequently, brands and companies are now vying for central positions inside consumer networks.

Consumers have become attracted to third-party information providers, through collaborative product reviews, ranking, rating, and price-comparison services. There are new and more complex concepts being applied to modern marketing. Lee Odden will help you craft new strategies and tactics in line with this new marketing environment.

In my capacity as chair of the SES Global Advisory Board, I'm honored to have Lee as a valuable member and supporter. I've watched him many times, either as a solo speaker or as a panelist at conferences. And without fail, when he begins to speak, keyboards begin to click as the audience takes note after note.

It's funny, but a classic movie scene popped into my mind after reading something Lee says in this book. It's from the movie *City Slickers*. Tough cowboy Curly (Jack Palance) holds up one finger, looks at Mitch (Billy Crystal), and says: "Do you know what the secret to life is?" Mitch replies, "Your finger?" "Just one thing," says Curly. "What's the one thing?" asks Mitch. To which Curly replies, "That's what *you* have to find out," and then gallops off into the distance.

I don't know about life, but when it comes to marketing and business, this book is about just one thing you can do to improve it: *Optimize!*

# Preface

At a large search marketing conference several years ago, I had a conversation with Maile Ohye from Google about public speaking, noting how impressive she was. As an active public speaker myself, I shared with her how I was able to get by with good information and enthusiasm, but without much polish. What she said next hit me like a ton of bricks: "You're an SEO and you optimize websites for better performance in search engines, right?" To which I replied yes. Her follow-up was, "Then why don't you optimize your speaking skills?"

Have you ever watched a movie where the camera is tight on a scene and, for dramatic effect, it pulls back in a blur? That's what I was feeling when Maile made her simple, yet powerful recommendation. What hit me wasn't just that I should work on my speaking skills, but the broader notion of optimization and how it applies to a persistent effort at improving just about anything for better performance.

## ADAPT OR DIE

Reading this book is a great first step toward a new way of thinking about how you can apply optimization principles to your business. The sheer volume of content created each day, coupled with the explosive growth of social media accessed on the Internet and on mobile and tablet devices, can be overwhelming. I've spent an incredible amount of time testing and making sense of the search and social web. My hope is that you'll find this book a quick study on the big-picture topics and deep on the practical resources for planning, implementing, and scaling a socialized and optimized content marketing strategy.

Millions of websites, with billions of pages and media, are indexed by search engines. Google alone handles more than 1 billion searches each day. A large number of the companies publishing information online that expect traffic from search engines have difficulty creating great content, let alone producing compelling content on a regular basis. Even companies that do create high-quality content often neglect how search engine optimization and social media marketing can expedite engagement between buyers and what the brand has to offer.

There's nothing static about Internet marketing, but the one constant we can all count on is the persistent effort by search engines to improve search quality and user experience. Such continuous improvements can affect how content is discovered, indexed, and sorted in search results as well as what external signals are considered to determine authority. Companies that ignore the current state of affairs with search technology and quality guidelines may feel the sting, as many website owners did with Google's Panda updates in 2011.

In addition to monitoring search engines, it's essential for results-oriented Internet marketing and communications professionals to understand the online information discovery, consumption, and engagement preferences of the people they're trying to reach. A better grasp of how customers find and seek out resources, the content topics and formats that motivate them, and the social media platforms and tools they use to engage and recommend things can be incredibly powerful for successful Internet marketing programs. Putting those insights into action means developing a proactive, adaptive, and integrated approach to content, search engine optimization, and social media marketing. Those companies that have adapted, such as Dell, Intel, and Zappos, have thrived. Businesses that have ignored the transformation of consumer trends and web technology have not fared so well.

## OPTIMIZED STATE OF MIND

Many companies treat their Internet marketing the same way I was treating my presentation skills. They get by with checklist SEO tactics, disconnected and difficult-to-measure social media marketing. On top of that, there's the challenge of creating high-quality content on a regular basis over a long period of time. If a company doesn't see the bigger-picture synergy of how to break social media, content, and SEO efforts out of departmental silos and approach Internet marketing and public relations holistically, how can they grow and remain competitive? To me, the notion of optimization is more about brands and customers than it is about keywords and rankings on search engines. Being "optimized" is a state of mind, and with this book, I hope to convert you into becoming more optimized in your marketing and communications.

If there's one thing I've learned over the past 14-plus years of working in the Internet marketing industry is the uncanny ability that high-performing SEO professionals have to use out-of-the-box creative, analytical, and lateral thinking to proactively solve marketing problems and find competitive advantages. At the same time, my work in the public relations field has shown me how messaging, influence, and engagement sync perfectly to help brands become the most relevant solution for their category, whether it's through search, social media, or other forms of online communications. The notion of search optimization might have a strong history with keywords, links, and pages in search engines, but an "optimize" mentality is a way of thinking that can give organizations like yours a competitive advantage in any area of a business that creates content online, from marketing and PR to customer service and human resources.

In that context, I encourage you to ask the same kinds of questions I pondered in my discussion with Maile, "Are your SEO, social media, and content marketing efforts optimized to work together? Are your marketing and communications optimized for specific audiences and outcomes?"

## THIS BOOK IS FOR YOU

This book is for the marketers, public relations professionals, small- to medium-sized business owners, and large company marketing executives who want to understand and implement a road map that incorporates the synergies of content, social media, and search engine optimization. In the three phases of this book, we build a crystal clear picture of how to plan, execute, and scale an integrated approach to social media optimization and content marketing.

### What This Book Will Teach You

- Phase 1 guides you in understanding the changing nature of consumer preferences and behaviors with search, social media, and content, as well as what that means for your online marketing strategy.
- Phase 2 explores optimized content marketing tactics from developing personas to social networking to content planning and measurement. We dig into key insights and examples of holistic search engine optimization for more effective search and social media marketing.
- Phase 3 is about scale and discusses processes and training you'll need to grow and maintain an integrated social media, SEO, and content marketing program in your organization.

Are you ready to get optimized? Let's get started.

# Acknowledgments

So much more goes into creating a book than anyone realizes, especially for a first-time author. Even though I've been blogging for over eight years and have written over 2,000 articles and blog posts on my own, writing a book is by no means a solitary activity. Numerous people contribute to the ideas, perspectives, and knowledge that come together in a book's creation. I've made many connections with amazingly smart, curious, and interesting people over many years of blogging, speaking at conferences, client consulting, and from being a participant on the social web at large. All the good people I've connected with have played a part in developing the point of view, insights, and perspectives shared in this book. For that I thank you all.

To our blog and newsletter subscribers, Facebook fans, Twitter followers, Google+ friends, and the TopRank Online Marking community on the web—I get to learn something new from our interactions every single day. Thank you for the opportunity to engage and learn together.

A very special thank you goes to Ashley Zeckman, who hit the ground running at TopRank Online Marketing and has been a true "right hand" during the most important phases of this book. Her tireless dedication helped make it possible. Thank you to all the members of the TopRank Online Marketing team, including Jolina Pettice and Mike Yanke who pitched in to help with *Optimize* and to my partner Susan Misukanis who provided support and took on additional responsibilities in order for me to write.

Numerous industry friends and peers were helpful during this process, some unknowingly. Thanks to authors Jay Baer, Ann Handley, Bryan Eisenberg, Mike Stelzner, Ron Jones, Greg Jarboe, Mike Moran, and Mike Grehan, who answered my questions, and offered encouragement and even fair warning about the before, during, and after of writing a book.

A tip of the hat goes to search, social media, and content marketing thought leaders who have been an inspiration to me for writing and the endless pursuit of knowledge in the online marketing and PR industries: Brian Clark, Chris Brogan, Brian Solis, Charlene Li, Michael Brito, David Meerman Scott, David Alston, Rebecca Lieb, John Jantsch, Danny Sullivan, Andy Beal, William Murray, Aaron Strout, Chuck Hemann, Katie Payne, Shonali Burke, Arik Hanson, Tac Anderson, Jason Falls, Brett Tabke, Rick Calvert, Heidi Cohen, Eric Schwartzman, Mel Carson, Vanessa Fox, Aaron Goldman, Avinash Kaushik, and Bill Hunt. Thanks to Chris Heuer for the spark many years ago that opened my mind to the world of social media. Thanks to Joe Pulizzi for bringing the rain of attention on content marketing—a rising tide lifts all ships, my friend.

Thank you to the editorial staff at Wiley and, in particular, the persistence and patience of Shannon Vargo, who saw potential where I didn't and proved to be a great compass in my book writing journey.

Books are written nights and weekends and that means sacrifices in time from my wife, Susan, and especially "the munchkins" Dominic, Cameron, and Violet. They are the inspiration for anything and everything good that I do.

Without family there is nothing, and so I must thank my parents, Michael and Ruthe, for their unconditional support, love, and enthusiasm.

# PHASE 1

# PLANNING

# CHAPTER 1

## Setting the Stage for an Optimized State of Mind

Several years ago my family established a tradition of celebrating the tenth birthday of each of our children by taking them on a trip to a city of their choosing somewhere in North America. My son Dominic picked New York City. While I travel to New York several times a year for business, I really had no idea what kid-friendly activities we could find for a five-day vacation in one of the world's greatest cities. Where did I go for advice and information? Some people reading this book will think of a search engine like Google or Bing. For others, Facebook or Twitter will come to mind. Some might even know specific people they could e-mail for travel tips or specialty travel websites that focus on New York. What did I do? I used all of these ideas.

I posted on Twitter that I would be bringing my son to New York for his tenth birthday and that we were looking for kid-friendly activities and places to see. Numerous suggestions were offered, and from them I made a list. Dominic and I used Google to research each destination and to find out details such as available activities, location, fees, and schedules. Based on what we found, we further refined our search phrases, which influenced follow-up questions posted on social networks. Some of the websites we found posted ratings from customers; others had links to blogs, photos on Flickr, and Facebook fan pages.

From our research conducted through a combination of search engines, social networking websites, and e-mail, we settled on our itinerary and had a fantastic time.

We didn't stop there, though. As we explored the city from Manhattan to the Bronx Zoo to Broadway to see *The Lion King*, I tweeted comments about our experiences and uploaded photos to Flickr, Twitter, and Facebook so the people who had made suggestions for our trip could see the impact they had on this once-in-a-lifetime experience. My social network experienced our adventures right along with us interacting, sharing, and engaging from all over the world. The content and media I posted online became findable on Google and has undoubtedly provided helpful ideas to others who are looking for information on kid-friendly activities in New York for years to come.

Our experience in planning that trip to New York with content discovered through search and social media represents a fundamental change that's emerged in consumer behaviors for information discovery, consumption, and engagement. While search engines continue to represent the most popular method of finding specific information, the influence of social networking, shared social media, and the proliferation of platforms for individuals to publish content all intersect to create tremendous opportunities to better attract and engage customers.[1] Recognizing the importance, relevance, and need to master each of these changing consumer preferences is essential for businesses to succeed online.

## CONTENT MARKETING TRILOGY: DISCOVERY, CONSUMPTION, AND ENGAGEMENT

The web is flush with change and innovation. Gone are the days of linear information flow and incremental growth. Content flows in every direction through a variety of platforms, formats, and devices. The mass adoption of the social and mobile web has facilitated a revolution of information access, sharing, and publishing at a scale never before experienced. (See Figure 1.1.)

Access to information for discovery is most often associated with search engines. For people who have some idea of what they want or need, it's second nature to search and then sort through the results for

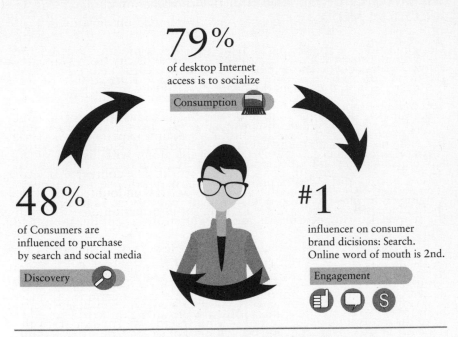

**FIGURE 1.1** Discovery, Consumption, and Engagement

the best answer. When my eight-year-old points to the Google Chrome browser icon on a computer desktop, she doesn't call it Google or Chrome. She calls it "the Internet," because it represents the interface she uses to search and connect with information online. For her, Internet access isn't thought of as anything special and certainly is not limited to a computer. Her perception of information transcends devices, whether a smart phone, an iPad, a PlayStation 3, an Apple TV, or a laptop. Just as she is growing up in a digital age where information access is ubiquitous, companies and their customers are "growing up" digitally and finding a wealth of opportunities to connect and engage.

While search plays an important part in how we connect with what we need online, the revolution occurring on the social web has had a global impact, from neighborhoods to entire nations. Recognizing the synergies of search and social media plus the role they play with content marketing will help businesses realize the impact on their ability to connect, engage, and grow revenue.

## THE INTERSECTION OF SEARCH OPTIMIZATION AND SOCIAL MEDIA

Google handles a staggering 11 billion queries a month.[2] But did you know Twitter delivers more than 350 billion tweets each day?[3] Facebook has nearly 1 billion users, and Google Plus is likely to reach more than 100 million users in 2012.[4,5]

With two in three adults using social networks, social media is hot, but is by no means mutually exclusive of search.[6] The notion of search has expanded beyond Google and Bing, and marketers from companies of all sizes and industries must now consider other search channels, ranging from internal Facebook search to innovations such as Siri on the iPhone 4S, as opportunities for content creation, optimization, and social promotion.

The blur of all this change is an opportunity for brands and marketers to engage in an active marketing strategy that converges the disciplines of search, social media, content, and online public relations. To meet brand needs to engage customers in an always-on digital world, whether it's B2B or B2C, the convergence of marketing and public relations, search, and social media are inevitable.

Because there are so many information sources online, sales cycles are getting longer. Customers expect more than to be presented with features and benefits followed by a call to action.

For marketers, more isn't always better. Relevance, timeliness, and ease of sharing are better. That means better content and visibility in all the places customers might be looking or might be influenced by. It also means a better experience with brand and consumer interactions.

For example, searchers expect not only to find what they're looking for on a search engine, but also to interact with what they find through commenting, rating, joining, as well as buying. Purchase is just the start of social engagement with the customer, which extends across a life cycle that takes the customer from prospect to evangelist. Adaptive Internet marketing pays attention to those customer needs and creates a dynamic cycle of social and search interaction.

Creating experiences that are easily discovered through search or social media and continuously evaluating what works and what doesn't helps to fuel the most critical aspects of an effective editorial, optimization, and social media marketing effort.

## WHATEVER CAN BE SEARCHED CAN BE OPTIMIZED

There's nothing static about Internet marketing, but the one constant we can all count on is the persistent effort by search engines to improve search quality and user experience. Such continuous improvements, including the Google Search, plus Your World implementation in late 2011, have significantly affected how search engines interact with content ranging from discovery, indexation, sorting in search results, to what external signals are considered to determine authority.

It's essential for results-oriented marketers to monitor both the front- and back-end landscapes of search to be proactive about what it will take to achieve and maintain a competitive advantage. Continuous efforts toward progressive search strategy for marketers are important, because we cannot rely on Google to send us "Weather Reports" every time an update is made.

In 2007, Google and other search engines like Ask.com made some of the most significant changes ever, affecting search results by including more sources such as Images, Maps, Books, Video, and News for certain queries.[7] In an effort to capitalize on the opportunity for improved search visibility for the array of media types included in search results, concepts like Digital Asset Optimization came about.[8]

Fast-forward to 2011 and you'll find that search results have evolved from 10 blue links to situationally dependent mixed-media results that vary according to your geographic location, web history, social influences, and social ratings like Google+. At any given time there are from 50 to 200 different versions of Google's core algorithm in the wild, so the notion of optimizing for a consistently predictable direct cause and effect is long gone.[9]

The potential influence of social media sites such as Twitter and Facebook with Google, Bing, and Yahoo! as link sources has changed what it means to build links for SEO and how we view whether PageRank is still important. (See Figure 1.2.) Social signals are rich sources of information for search engines, and old ways of link acquisition simply don't have the same effect in the same ways.

As the world's most popular search engine, Google says its mission is to "Organize the world's information and make it universally accessible and useful." Marketers need to understand the opportunities to make information—including various types of digital assets—easy for

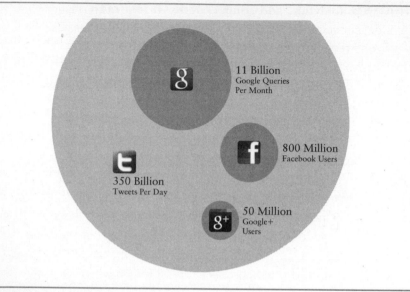

**FIGURE 1.2    Channel of Discovery: Search and Social Networks**

search engines to find, index, and sort in search results. Structured data in the form of markup, microformats, and rich snippets, as well as feeds and sitemaps, all play an increasingly important role in helping Google achieve this goal.

At the same time, so does understanding myriad data sources and file types that can be included in search results. By understanding these opportunities, search marketers can inventory their digital assets and deploy a better, more holistic SEO strategy that realizes the benefit of inclusion and visibility where customers are looking.

Increasingly, marketers are approaching search optimization holistically under the premise, "What can be searched can be optimized." That means more attention is being paid to the variety of reasons people search as well as the variety of reasons companies publish digital content. Content and SEO are perfect partners for making it easy to connect constituents and customers with brand content.

In the past, SEO consultants have typically been left to deal with whatever content they could optimize and promote for link building. Now the practice of SEO involves content creation and curation as much as it does with reworking existing content. When SEO practitioners examine the search results page of targeted keyword phrases on a regular basis, review web analytics, and conduct social media monitoring, they can gain a deeper sense of what new sources and content types can be leveraged for better search visibility.

Monitoring search results might show that the keyword terms being targeted may trigger different types of content. Certain search queries might be prone to triggering images and video, not just web pages. An understanding of the search results landscape for a target keyword phrase should be considered when allocating content creation and keyword optimization resources.

For many companies, it can be very difficult and complex to implement a holistic content marketing and search optimization program. Substantial changes may be necessary with content creation, approval, and publishing processes. But the upside is that a substantial increase in the diversity of content and media types indexed and linking to a company website will provide the kind of advantage standard SEO no longer offers.

As long as there are search engines, and search functionality on websites, there will be some kind of optimization for improving marketing performance of content in search. Companies need to consider all the digital assets, content, and data they have to work with to give both search engines and customers the information they're looking for in the formats they'll respond to.

## OPTIMIZE FOR CUSTOMERS

No doubt, you've searched Google or Bing and found web pages that were clearly "optimized" in the name of SEO. That kind of copy might help a page appear higher in search results but doesn't do much for readers once they click through.

When I see those pages, it reminds me of the increasing importance of optimizing for customers and user experience versus the common overemphasis on search engines. Keep in mind, technical SEO and understanding how bots interact with servers and web pages are timeless best practices, but it just makes sense to write web copy that's more useful and a better reflection of what customers are looking for versus chasing the most popular keywords alone. (See Figure 1.3.)

I recall reading an SEO blog a long time ago that advised creating websites, copy, and links as though search engines didn't exist. That seems a bit naive—especially if you're in a competitive category. Creating,

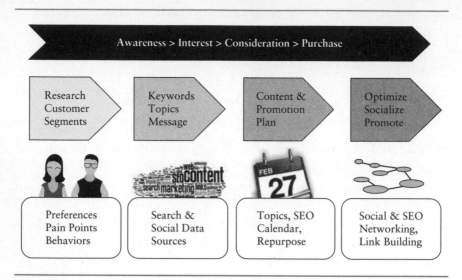

**FIGURE 1.3    Optimize For Customers**

optimizing, and promoting content based on customers' interests that leads them to a purchase makes the most out of both useful content and SEO best practices. Great SEO copywriting doesn't read as a list of keywords, but instead balances keyword usage with creative writing that appeals to the reader, thus educating, influencing, and inspiring action.

Consider the difference between these general SEO copywriting recommendations:

> Use the most popular keywords at the beginning of title tags, in on-page titles, body copy, anchor text, and image alt text in combination with attracting relevant keyword links from other websites so the pages rank high on Google. Higher-ranking web pages can result in more visitors and sales.

In comparison, try this advice, which is absent any explicit SEO lingo:

> Use the words that matter most to your customers in titles, links, and body copy to inform and inspire them to take action. Text used in titles should make it easy for readers to understand the topic of the page quickly, in the first few words. Text used to link from one page to another should give the readers an idea of what they'll find on the

destination page. A consistent approach to titling, label-
ing, and copy in web page text, image annotations, video
descriptions, and links will create confidence for the reader
in the subject matter and inspire sales.

Both recommendations should result in more focused and relevant
content for search engines. But the focus in the first instance is only on
keywords and search engines. The advice in the second instance is less SEO-
specific, but emphasizes relevance from the customer point of view and at
the same time is search engine–friendly. Marketers need to take a step back
and review which audience and outcomes they're optimizing for: search
engines and rankings or customers and sales. What about all of the above?

## OPTIMIZE FOR EXPERIENCES

My friend Bob Knorpp had a good piece about the fallacy of content in
*Advertising Age*, "Why Marketers Should Break Free of the Digital Content
Trap." He made some good points about companies going through the
motions of creating and promoting content on social channels with motivations of retweets, likes, shares, and links instead of real engagement. I have to
agree when he says, "Content alone is a dead end for ongoing engagement."

Savvy online marketers don't see content as a shortsighted substitute
for social strategy or simply as an SEO tactic but as a proxy to creating
better customer experiences. Content is the mechanism for storytelling,
and if social and search optimization are also involved in a qualitative
way to aid in discovery and sharing of those stories, then all the better.

In that *Ad Age* article, Bob also makes great points about the need to
think of new ways to approach digital storytelling beyond single dimensions
like videos that go viral and infographics that spread like wildfire on Twitter
and Facebook. Engagement is indeed more than a click, a share, or a link.

In the same way that many business bloggers and marketers approach
online marketing with an egocentric perspective, promoting messages in
which they try to persuade audiences instead of empathizing with customer needs and interests, many agencies that create content are more
interested in creative self-expression than in experiences that are truly
meaningful to customers.

In our hub/spoke and constellation publishing models for content marketing (covered more in-depth in Chapter 8), we emphasize

an understanding of customer needs and behaviors through persona development and attention to variances during the buying cycle. Those insights, combined with ongoing monitoring and engagement, drive content marketing strategy and the creative mix of content objects designed to help prospects have meaningful experiences with the brand.

The content itself is made easier to discover in more relevant ways through search engine optimization and social media optimization. A "socialize and optimize" approach to content marketing increases the connections between consumers who are looking (i.e., searching) and discussing (social networking) topics of relevance to the brand solution.

I've said it before: Great content isn't great until it's discovered, consumed, and shared. Littering the social web with scheduled tweets, status updates, and blog posts alone is not engagement, and it certainly does not create the kind of experience that builds brand or motivates customers to buy, be loyal, or advocate.

## ARE YOU READY TO BE OPTIMIZED?

From an overall marketing and customer engagement perspective, all content is not created equal. Any kind of content isn't appropriate in any kind of situation, despite what recent content marketing SEO advocates would have you believe. Since much of the focus of online marketing is on customer acquisition, many SEO efforts emphasize transaction or lead generation outcomes. That's what they're held accountable for. Unfortunately, search to purchase or social to purchase are not the only ways people interact with information online. Research before purchase and education and support afterward are also important.

Being in the "brand as publisher" business is better than not creating any content at all, but it's a much more effective thing to be purposeful in content creation and marketing according to the full customer experience. Seeing content engagement opportunities holistically can provide a company more ways to initiate, maintain, and enhance customer relationships.

For example, in the context of online marketing, there are many different touch points during the customer relationship. Using the buying cycle model of Awareness, Consideration, Purchase, Service, and Loyalty, marketers can best plan what kind of content may be most appropriate to engage customers according to their needs.

For a holistic editorial plan, here are a few types of content and methods of communication to consider:

**Awareness**

- Public relations
- Advertising
- Word of mouth
- Social media

**Consideration**

- Search marketing
- Advertising
- Social media
- Webinars
- Product and service reviews
- Blogs
- Direct response

**Purchase**

- Website
- Social commerce

**Service**

- Social media
- Social CRM
- Online messaging
- E-mail
- Search

**Loyalty**

- E-mail newsletter
- Webinars
- Blog
- Social network, forum—community

In the development of a content marketing strategy, there are numerous opportunities to be more relevant and effective. Planning content that's meaningful to the customers you're trying to engage according to where they are in the buying cycle and overall customer relationship provides greater efficiency in content creation and in the repurposing of content.

Holistic content marketing and editorial planning also help make better use of tactics that transcend the relationship timeline, like SEO and social media. It's especially the case with holistic SEO that content producers can extend their reach and visibility to customers who are looking not just to buy, but to engage with brands in other ways.

By considering the content needs across the customer life cycle, not just acquisition or conversion, companies can become significantly more effective and efficient in their ability to connect relevant messages and stories with customers who are interested. The result: shorter sales cycles, better customer relationships, and more word of mouth.

Now we've set the stage for an "optimized" approach to search, social, and content marketing. Chapter 2 digs into where this mind-set fits for B2B, B2C, small and large companies, as well as within specific business functional areas ranging from marketing to customer service. Let's get optimized!

## ACTION ITEMS

1. Think about your current content, optimization, and social media marketing efforts. How could you start integrating those programs?
2. What areas of your content marketing could you start optimizing related to content discovery, consumption, and sharing?
3. Is your content optimization more focused on keywords or customers? Consider how you could begin to evaluate customer needs as inspiration for keyword research and content.
4. Look at your current social media content. Where might you begin to optimize for better social engagement and customer experience?
5. Identify the spectrum of content types used from the top of the buying cycle to customer support. Consider how you might optimize and socialize content more holistically.

# CHAPTER 2

## Journey: Where Does Optimize and Socialize Fit in Your Company?

Companies large and small, in industries from retail to manufacturing, publish content online with an expectation that a certain audience of people will find, read, and act on that content. While most search engine optimization and social media marketing efforts are rightly focused on marketing goals like acquiring more customers and increasing revenue, making purchases is not the only reason consumers use search or ask for referrals through social networks.

There's a lot of tactical advice online about search, social media, and content marketing for companies that want to better connect with customers, but that advice doesn't always consider the differences between types of companies or even content within companies. For the best return on marketing investment, it's important to understand that there are notable differences in tactics for effective optimization depending on the audience and how they prefer to discover, consume, and act on information. The very nature of B2C versus B2B or small company versus large company content, audience, and outcomes can be different, so the approach to optimizing content for search and social media must be tailored accordingly.

As an online marketer, you're charged with assessing internal resources, overall business goals, customer buying cycle, and time frame in order to make the best decisions possible with your resources. As you read on, watch for some of the things that best represent your business and online marketing situation. This chapter gives you optimization examples to understand the differences between B2B, B2C, small companies, and large companies. We will also talk about several rarely explored opportunities for holistic search and social media optimization of content: internal departments such as public relations, customer service, and human resources and recruiting.

## OPTIMIZED B2C SEARCH MARKETING

J&O Fabrics is a small business in New Jersey that was historically focused on selling fabric through its brick-and-mortar store as well as through online channels like eBay. Dissatisfaction with third-party marketing costs in combination with a frustration over limited website traffic led to an investment in SEO. As a result of optimizing the website with relevant keywords and a program designed to attract links, traffic to the J&O Fabrics website increased 214 percent. The company's online marketing became more efficient and effective, allowing it to eliminate certain types of advertising and increase organic "free" search traffic significantly.

Stop there and you have a typical SEO success story. But Ryan Safady of J&O Fabrics understood from the start that content was the key to making the pages of his online store stand out for more than just search engines. With a keen understanding of customer needs as well as data from web analytics and keyword research, content creation and optimization were made part of the process of maintaining product content on the website www.jandofabrics.com. As a small business, J&O needed to use their resources efficiently, so when a blog was started, an existing customer e-mail newsletter was leveraged for content along with a free blog-hosting platform. Knowing what types of products customers were prone to buy online and in which season helped flavor content and optimization efforts on a mix of broad topics and more specific long-tail keyword phrases. The combination of making keyword optimization a process for updating and adding new content to the online store as well as offering customer-centric tips on the blog helped facilitate a website that became highly relevant for ready-to-buy customers, search engines, and other websites that link to useful resources. Increased content relevancy and usefulness inspired the kind of inbound links and social sharing that search engines like Google reward with top three positions on hundreds of important keyword phrases. Extensive top search visibility has enabled J&O's small business to effectively compete directly with national chains, all based from a single retail store.

J&O Fabrics has continued to work on being the most relevant source of fabric online by expanding content and optimization efforts to Twitter, Facebook, and YouTube. Social channels share unique content with the J&O Fabrics community and involve members in content creation through contests and promotions that result in even more awareness, sharing, and links. A strong search and social media presence reinforces a cycle of discovery, consumption, and sharing that involves current customer networks as well as attracting new customers actively looking to purchase specific products.

## B2B CONTENT MARKETING OPTIMIZATION

Companies focused on business-to-business sales often experience a much longer sales cycle involving the creation of more content that serves to educate and nurture prospects into qualified leads and customers. In other words, there's usually a lot more content romance involved with B2B prospects before they become customers.

The approach to optimization for J&O Fabrics as a small, B2C company was notably different than that employed by Marketo, a B2B marketing software company. Before Marketo's initial product was officially launched, the company made the decision to invest in content and optimization, particularly through the practice of blogging. Whereas J&O Fabrics had a longstanding website and content to begin with, Marketo started its SEO efforts with a very new website and blog. B2B markets are often less competitive in search, but that was not the case with Marketo, which faced several longstanding competitors that had anywhere from 3 to 10 years' head start with their search engine optimization programs.

Audits are a key part of search engine optimization, allowing marketers to assess the current state of the website in ways that identify any conflicts or inefficiencies for search engines as they crawl, index, and rank web pages. An audit with Marketo's website early on helped chart a productive course toward technical optimization of the content management system as well as a content creation plan. Blogs can be highly effective players in an integrated search and social media strategy, and Marketo took full advantage of the platform by creating an intelligent and ambitious mix of keyword-rich content that was just as relevant to buyers as it was to search engines.

Keyword research into broad industry- and category-focused keyword phrases that would associate Marketo as an industry player, in combination with more specific phrases relevant to buyers as they make their way through the sales process, played well for Marketo in its SEO and content creation efforts. Beginning as a small business and a start-up, Marketo has been able to accelerate the growth of its business through the marketing efficiency and effectiveness that come from content and search engine optimization focused both on customers and search engines.

The result? Although Marketo is only a four-year-old company in the B2B marketing space, you can easily find the company on Google using phrases like "B2B Marketing" in a category where competitors have operated full-scale SEO programs for nearly 10 years. One keyword doesn't make a business, though, and Marketo understands that an abundance of information online means prospects have pulled themselves through much of the traditional sales funnel by discovering and consuming brand content. Marketo's dedication to creating and promoting relevant content on its array of blogs and resource center in accordance to the information needs of its prospects throughout the buying cycle facilitated a substantial online presence on hundreds of competitive topics where the company's prospective customers were actively looking. In fact, Marketo added more than 1,100 customers[1] in its first three years, and revenue increased 700 percent over a two-year period, with vice president of marketing Jon Miller citing search and blogging as being the most effective lead-generation tactics[2] during an Online Marketing Summit conference in San Diego.

## OPTIMIZATION AND THE ENTERPRISE

Large and complex organizations have many more considerations with coordinated optimization, social media, and content marketing efforts. Many effective SEO and social media marketing consultants have had difficulty making an impact because of their inability to win internal client support among interdepartmental teams needed for implementation. Competent SEO and social media marketing expertise is moot if a consultant doesn't understand how to navigate large and complex organizational structures. Success is as dependent on political and organizational savvy as it is on content marketing mastery.

A very large company in the health care technology field, which generates tens of billions of dollars in annual revenue among more than 20 different companies, decided to roll all of the disparate company brands and websites under a common corporate content management system. Customers visiting the old website addresses were redirected to the new home of the company under the main company website. The new CMS allowed centralized management of website resources and a common brand identity.

The company soon realized that, although the combined website presented a unified brand and redirected requests for old pages to new destinations, the methods of redirection were not as easy for search engines to understand as they were for people. Website traffic was affected and an SEO audit was completed to identify the issues that we significantly affecting organic search engine traffic. Working with more than 20 different business and operating units as well as corporate IT, the SEO migration issues were identified and a range of SEO best practices recommendations implemented in order to provide search engines a crystal clear signal of what was old, what was new. As a result, search engines were better able to see and rank the most relevant pages without confusion while continuing to provide a good user experience for customers that clicked on old links.

Seeing an even bigger opportunity, the company decided to further leverage search engine optimization as an effective method for relevant discovery and engagement with its B2B prospects. An SEO program was rolled out among individual business units with the corporate website and public relations content. Ongoing SEO implementation, content creation, link building, and formal and informal training resulted in significant increases in search traffic and online leads across the portfolio of companies.

Because this company is one of the largest in the world, change isn't always easy to implement, but the SEO consulting and training initiatives grew confidence in online marketing programs, and the company has been implementing more social media components into its online marketing mix along with content and optimization. Confidence in the technical and creative aspects of SEO and content combined with multi-department and business unit training on best practices helped this 150+-year-old company transition into more integrated SEO and content marketing processes before many of their competitors.

## PUBLIC RELATIONS

When social media participation by brands became more popular, companies often began with marketing and sales outcomes in mind but soon discovered that people use social tools for many types of communication ranging from customer service to public relations to recruiting. The same opportunity exists with optimizing content for easy and relevant discovery through search engines.

The content that marketing departments produce is not the only type of information that can be optimized. Many other areas of an organization publish content online for specific audience and outcomes. The public relations function within a company often produces nearly as much content as marketing in the form of a corporate newsroom with media coverage, press releases, images, video, case studies, white papers, and other resources that would be useful to journalists. Each of those assets is an opportunity for journalists to discover the brand story through search engines or social referrals.

PRWeb is a press release distribution service that publishes thousands of press releases for PR practitioners and small business marketers every month. As a pioneer in the area of optimized press release distribution, PRWeb has been relied on by the SEO and PR industries to deliver outcomes such as high-ranking press releases on Google and Yahoo! News, website traffic, and links for more than 10 years. Companies that optimize and socialize their press releases give new life and extended reach to their news by making it easy for bloggers and end consumers to find and share press release content.

When it comes to integrating SEO, social media, and content with public relations, PRWeb walks the talk by producing industry reports, blogging, and managing a robust resource section on their website with numerous optimized articles that are helpful to their target audience, including journalists. Additionally, PRWeb leverages social media channels such as Facebook, LinkedIn, and Twitter to connect with their community. PRWeb community manager Stacey Acevero holds Twitter chats every other week (called #PRWebchat) that brings together prospects, customers, bloggers, and the media to ask and answer questions along a theme and often including a guest subject matter expert. With an editorial plan that factors search keywords in place, web and social media content produced and promoted by PRWeb is more likely to be found in search; and with increasing numbers of journalists reporting search as a tool they use daily, it makes SEO an excellent public relations resource. Jason DeRusha, News Anchor for WCCO-TV, supports this notion of search as a PR asset, "I begin every day at search engine. It doesn't matter what story I'm working on, it always starts with a search."

Within the public relations department arsenal of content, there's a mix of optimization opportunities beyond the press release, from the corporate newsroom to video and images to social media content and even contributed articles to publications and blogs. The unique opportunity for PR content optimization is that it serves the information needs of the news media as well as end consumers.

## CUSTOMER SERVICE

While much of the optimization and social media efforts of companies is focused on content related to customer acquisition, there's tremendous value in making sure content that serves existing customers is easy to find. That means optimizing frequently asked questions and other support material for easy and relevant discovery through search. From a social media perspective, it means being aware of which support-related search queries are most popular so that topical social media monitoring efforts can uncover service opportunities on platforms like Twitter, in forums, or in comments on blogs. Customer support web page optimization also affects social content creation, so answers are easily discovered and shared within social channels by social media community managers, customer service staff, and brand advocates.

Optimization of content for customer discovery can happen with public information that's accessed via search engines like Google or Bing as well as internal repositories of information behind a login. A large health care technology company faced the need to optimize post-sale content for customers. Feedback from usability studies showed that customers were having trouble locating information, such as frequently asked questions and user information, in the customer portal.

To help provide a better customer experience, SEO best practices were applied to existing content to create better content architecture and ensure relevant results were served via the search functionality of the internal customer portal. The project began by identifying customer segments and working with client-side marketers and customer service reps to identify the information customers were most likely to search for.

Next, a separate keyword glossary was researched and created for the content found within the customer portal. Following the development of the keyword glossary, best-practice search engine optimization was applied, including editing titles of documents, headings, copy, and cross-linking within copy.

The end result was better-organized, easier-to-find content to help serve customer needs across multiple post-sale stages.

Making customer content easier to navigate and find quickly can lead to increased customer satisfaction, increased frequency of accessing customer focused resources, and, ultimately, cost savings by displacing inquiries to a call center to the web.

## RECRUITING AND HR

Even with an uncertain economy, many companies have difficulty finding new employees who have the right mix of necessary skills. The recruiting industry has effectively used social media channels for promoting open positions and networking with candidates. Some companies have used Facebook, LinkedIn, and Twitter as part of their recruiting efforts. Ernst & Young was the first professional services firm to launch a careers page on Facebook in 2006 and now has a community of more than 50,000 fans there.[3] Talented people search the web, social networks, and job sites and to find something that catches their attention. Why not your company's job listing?

The Public Relations Society of America (PRSA), headquartered in New York, has maintained a job listing service that provides a useful source of career opportunities and advice for PR and communications professionals for several years. The PRSA jobcenter also serves as a resource for agencies and corporate PR departments that want to attract talented candidates. By reviewing website traffic trends and having keyword research performed, William Murray, president and COO of the PRSA, decided SEO was worth exploring to help the jobcenter content and job listings attract more search engine traffic, thereby creating additional value for the companies that paid to list job openings there. After SEO work was performed related to job listing keyword research, a website audit, content audit, and link-building program were implemented. Total traffic to the PRSA site increased by 20 percent, while page views for the PRSA jobcenter increased by 40 percent. Additionally, visitor referrals from competitive keyword rankings increased substantially. Referrals from a single target keyword phrase with more than 76,200,000 competing search results on Google increased by over 450 percent.

If search engines like Google and Bing are imperfect, then the search functions within company websites are far from perfect. That means optimizing content for internal use can help employees (just like customers) find answers more quickly and efficiently. I'm sure many people reading this book have used Google or Bing to search for content on their own company website. That experience shows the power of a search engine for exposing content that's important for performing one's job. It also reveals the importance of making any kind of content with a purpose and an expected audience to be optimized for discovery through search.

Whether your small or large business is focused on B2B or B2C markets, it is essential to take advantage of the opportunity to optimize and socialize content to aid in the connection with intended audiences. Further, being able to discern the uniqueness of different customer expectations for how brand content is discovered, consumed, and acted on will help marketers better plan their content optimization and social media efforts to the benefit of customers and brands alike.

Now that we have an understanding of where an optimized approach can fit in with content marketing across marketing, public relations, recruiting, and customer service, let's move on to research in Chapter 3: From the search and social media landscape to the search engine–friendliness of your website.

## ACTION ITEMS

1. B2C companies: Identify product groups which have promising revenue opportunity that are not currently driving substantial search traffic as an optimization opportunity.

2. B2B companies: Take inventory of the different types and topics of content used to educate prospects during the buying cycle. Think about where those topics are being discussed on the social web and searched for on sites like Google, Yahoo, or Bing.

3. Small businesses: What is the most important thing you want your customers to know about your brand through a search engine? Make a plan to be the most relevant source of information online for that thing.

4. Large companies: What area of your business could you use to develop a business case for substantial improvement of search and social media visibility for your prospects? To your customers, employees, and industry news media?

5. Identify one or two key areas outside of marketing within your organization where improved search and social visibility could increase value, reduce costs, or positively affect revenue.

# CHAPTER 3

## Smart Marketing Requires Intelligence: Research, Audit, and Listen

Long before an army goes into battle, intelligence organizations are busy collecting and analyzing information about the opposing threat. The right information and insight could lead to a much more advantageous outcome. Inaccurate information or an absence of competitive research can lead to disaster.

In the competitive world of content marketing, search, and social media optimization, it's essential for companies of all sizes and industries to understand their online marketplace in order to gain a business advantage and develop a competitive strategy. This chapter covers several key areas of assessment, including the search and social landscape and website SEO readiness.

The approach to competitive search and social media research can vary widely by situation, but it's essentially always going to involve some kind of information capture, assessment, and comparison. A new business entering a competitive market with companies that have mature Internet marketing programs may need to uncover key weaknesses in their competitors' marketing efforts in order to compete "David and Goliath" style. In a situation with companies that have very similar levels of Internet marketing resources and effort, competitive research may uncover weaknesses or unrealized opportunities that can create advantage. In all cases, an understanding of the competitive search and social media landscape will help content marketers differentiate to better attract and engage with customers.

In my many years of online marketing experience, I've seen a wide variety of companies enter the web marketing space with different ideas about what's possible as well as different levels of understanding about what or who their competition really is. For example, one entrepreneur in the self-help area of memory and IQ improvement offering online puzzles as content wanted an SEO program that would help achieve top visibility on Google for the term "brain." With a new website and nearly 700 million competing search results for the search term, a first-glance evaluation indicated the desired outcome to be unlikely with any reasonable budget and time frame. Further competitive research into the search landscape did not reveal the list of online puzzle and learning websites considered by the entrepreneur to be competitors, but rather a mix of Wikipedia, university (Harvard), industry publication, and resource websites with large numbers of web pages and a long history of search relevance for the topic. In the search and social media marketing world, the competition isn't always who you think. Companies need to understand that online competition isn't just made up of companies competing for market share in the business world, but also information and content published from a variety of sources that compete for search engine and social media users' attention.

In the case of the "brain" customer, thoughtful analysis of the search and social media landscape revealed popular forums and social networking groups focused on topics related to what the target website visitor would find useful. A more diverse yet more relevant keyword mix related to puzzles proved to be more attainable and, more important, a better reflection of the interests among the target community. A larger group of keyword targets promoted through the optimization of content and social media channels resulted in the entrepreneur's website reaching more than 300,000 unique visitors per month and a decision to change the business model to advertising over product sales because of the volume of traffic. Had the entrepreneur focused only on the term "brain" without conducting competitive and marketplace research, the company might still be selling just a few learning games and puzzles per month instead of having a thriving website supported by an active social community and strong search engine traffic.

## BUSINESS AND CONTENT COMPETITORS IN SEARCH RESULTS

There are many preconceived notions about what can be achieved with a good SEO program, and before companies allocate substantial resources, there should be an effort to understand the competitive landscape. With search engines, the competition can come in several forms, including search results, advertisements, social recommendations, digital assets, and links. Essentially, competition is anything that takes the attention of your prospects and customers away from your content. (See Figure 3.1.)

For the purpose of this book and its emphasis on content marketing, I discuss two approaches to competitive research with regard to search results. The first is based on the results pages for the keyword mix that you're after. Search engine results pages (SERPs) help answer the question about which business competitors and what types of content competition show up on the first page for the keyword phrases that you're targeting. This is an ongoing task performed monthly to identify trends or variances.

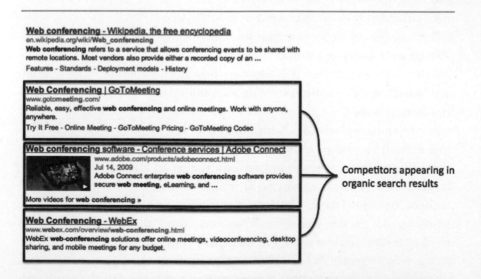

**FIGURE 3.1    Competitors Appearing in Organic Search Results**

The other approach is to monitor the search visibility of real-world competitors. With brick-and-mortar businesses, offline competitors are often quite different than online competitors who rank well for target keyword phrases. It can be useful to track offline competitors regardless of their position to see if they catch on to the value of SEO and experience a jump in search visibility. Of course, for an Internet-based business, all competitors are online. A useful tool for monitoring competitor organic keyword visibility on Google is SEMRush.

Monitoring the search results real estate for your brand, products, and services starts with keywords. If you have an idea of the most relevant phrases that represent your products and services mix, test queries on a search engine like Google or Bing to reveal some of your online competitors. We get a lot deeper into keyword research in Chapter 7, but for your preliminary efforts, a category-level understanding of keyword competitors within search will be a useful starting point. A tool like Google AdWords Keyword tool can help clarify whether your assumptions about keyword phrases are on target in terms of popularity and competitiveness. Once you identify a hit list of keyword phrases, review the search results pages on Google or Bing while you're not logged in to identify what types of business and content competitors appear. If you are logged in to Gmail, Google Analytics, Google+, or any other service from Google, the search results you see can be significantly different because of personalization from your web history and friends' Google+ shares.

Periodically revisit the search results for your most important keyword phrases, and document rankings as well as the makeup of content in the search results. (See Figure 3.2.) As you look at the different types of content in each search position over time, you may notice trends that reveal new opportunities.

For example, a trending story may cause news or blog results to appear high on the page, which might prompt you to comment on a high-ranking story or reach out to a journalist or blogger to offer your point of view. There's a great book you can download on Kindle called *Newsjacking* (by David Meerman Scott) that explores this practice in depth. Here's another example: When you notice that the search engine tends to favor certain media, such as video content, for one of your target keyword phrases, it may prompt you to focus on video content and optimization for a particular target keyword phrase with the intention of leveraging the perceived bias toward that type of media.

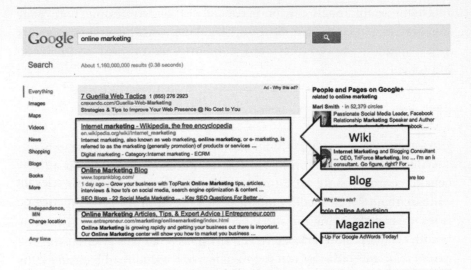

**FIGURE 3.2   Different Content Types Appearing in Organic Search Results**

Google, Yahoo, and Bing search result fluctuations for the same keyword phrase tracked over time do occur, with content types ranging from web pages to images to video. For both competitive research and opportunistic reasons, it makes sense to monitor the content mix of search results pages over time. There are also changes with how search engines display information that warrant attention to SERPs. For example. Google used to offer "real-time" search results on some queries with information syndicated from social media sites like Twitter. After launching Google+, and the lack of continued relationship with Twitter, Google stopped displaying those real-time search results, meaning it was no longer possible to use Twitter to gain near-instant search visibility on certain keyword phrases.

Monitoring the makeup of search results for keyword phrases that are relevant and in use by customers will help keep you apprised of overall search results competition as well as changes made by search engines in how they represent web content from their indexes.

Keep in mind, there's no getting around personalization if you're logged in to a search engine, and even if you're not logged in, search results can be personalized by your geographic location. Despite that, a relative measure over time of the search results pages that represent your most important topics can be beneficial for understanding both your business and content competition. Tracking what you're up against will help guide the right keyword, content planning, and optimization approach.

## RESEARCH THE SOCIAL LANDSCAPE

Customers are increasingly influenced by a combination of search and social media content. A study cited by eMarketer indicated that 48 percent of consumers are led to make a purchase through a combination of search and social media influences.[1] Understanding where conversations are happening on the social web relevant to the competition, your brand, products, and services as well as topics related to your customers, employees, and industry can help guide your social media strategy for content and engagement. (See Figure 3.3.)

There are a number of benefits for monitoring competitors on the social web, according to David Alston, CMO at Radian6, a salesforce. com company:[2]

> If you are watching your industry and the keywords used to describe it you will probably be the first to know when a new competitor appears on the scene. From a competitive

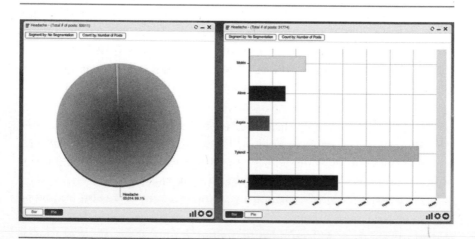

FIGURE 3.3    Radian6 Social Media Monitoring

intelligence perspective you may also wish to be alerted any time a competitor's name is used. Knowing this may highlight opportunities to reach out to potential customers who have indicated they are trialing a competitor or dissatisfied with a competitor's product or service. You may also discover which industry players are advocates for competitive brands giving you the opportunity to reach out and see if they are interested in knowing more about what you have to offer. Competitors will also often talk about subjects they are strategically interested in and being able to stay on top of those discussions allows you to anticipate potential future moves.

For the purpose of basic social media research, there are a few useful free social search tools (e.g., socialmention.com, search.twitter.com, or topsy.com) that can reveal useful information about topics of interest to your social media–savvy audience and about your competition. Twitter alone is very useful for mining information about sales and customer service opportunities, plus a whole host of other types of dialog and inquiry that are relevant to why your business communicates online ranging from competitive research to recruiting new employees.

There are a wide array of social media monitoring tools that can help identify threads of discussion that are relevant to your content and online marketing efforts. Basic tools like Andy Beal's Trackur provide a good starting point for organized, qualitative social media monitoring that also offers more advanced options as your needs expand. Other effective social media monitoring tools that vary in advanced features and price points include Alterian SM2, Lithium, and Radian6 from salesforce.com.

Once you decide on a measurement tool, the next step is to set up monitoring. Social media listening tools are keyword-based, so it's important to get a good handle on the unique throttling and filtering capabilities of the listening tool you're using to fine-tune the quality of social search results. Without using features like negative keywords, segmenting which channels to listen to and adjusting the degree of influence on different types of signals, you may end up getting a report full of blog spam instead of good sample representative of real discussions about relevant topics on the social web.

Some of the key insights that come from initial social listening and research include answers to the following questions:

- Is your category of product or service or your industry being discussed? What questions do people have? What are their concerns? What opportunities are being revealed?
- Is your brand being discussed, and what are people saying? Who is saying it, and where? What is the sentiment?
- What topics relevant to your specific business solutions are being discussed?
- Are any rogue employees publishing blogs or other social content without sanction or support from corporate marketing and public relations departments?
- On which social channels or websites are there active discussions and communities of interest relevant to your customer interests?
- Who are the influencers participating in key topic discussions and in what channels?
- Are your competitors' companies, products, and services being discussed, and where?
- Are your competitors active participants on the social web with content? What type of content?

After you've completed your initial monitoring to identify a baseline for conversations about social topics, competitors, and your brand and products, it's time to establish some ongoing monitoring of those conversations. Any of the tools just mentioned can help you perform this task. The important thing is to start with something fundamental, such as industry, brand, and competitor topics. Then grow the array of monitoring efforts according to your needs. Companies usually experiment with social media monitoring themselves, since there are a good number of tools that are easy to use. As social media monitoring needs grow, outside or dedicated resources are usually allocated in order to scale efforts beyond initial marketing objectives. Some companies add social media listening responsibilities to the duties of a social media strategist; others expand social listening into a full-team effort, complete with social media listening command centers (e.g., companies like Dell and Gatorade).[3,4]

One point of opportunity with search keywords and social media topics is to create a fixed and dynamic keyword list to determine whether any of the popular and relevant search phrases overlap with the social topics being discussed on social media websites. We dig more deeply into what you can do with that keyword insight in Chapters 7 to 11, but being able to find search keywords and social topics that overlap can be powerful guides for an optimized and socialized content marketing strategy. Content relevant for high search visibility that also caters to popular social topics can encourage social sharing, which in turn creates signals that reinforce better search visibility.

## TECHNICAL SEO AUDIT OF YOUR WEBSITE

Now it's time for the direction of our research to turn inward. There's more to this piece of the content marketing puzzle than marketplace and competitor research, including insight that could provide essential information for a website that is optimized for keywords and search engines as much as it's optimized for customers. Content marketing is a central theme to this book, but without visibility where customers and other target audiences are looking, search engines in particular, content efforts can fall flat or not reach their full potential. What can you do for significant improvement of your content search visibility? The answer to that question starts with a technical SEO audit.

Search engine optimization is a bit of a moving target involving a mix of influences. According to Google Webmaster Central, more than 200 variables are used when ranking web content.[5] The famous PageRank is just one of them. Google's Inside Search website states that it has anywhere between 50 and 200 versions of its core algorithm in the wild, so the notion of SEO professionals reverse-engineering Google's method of ranking web pages with universal predictability are gone.[6] However, what we can do is understand Google's and Bing's motivation for search quality and the emphasis on providing relevant answers fast. Search engines' algorithmic efforts are meant to produce not only the right information for searchers, but also the best user experience. Understanding how those motivations and the technical nature of search engines work is what helps content marketers plan, optimize, and promote content that is relevant for both search engines and customers.

Best-practices search engine optimization involves a mix of attention to keywords, content, links, social signals, and, increasingly, factors like page speed, the use of semantic markup, and author authority. When I'm asked for the one SEO tactic I'd always start with first or that I would recommend above all others, it would be a technical SEO audit. If a search engine can't make a copy of your website to show in the search results, then your site may as well not exist when it comes to expecting traffic from search engines. No pages in the search index would be like showing up to play a baseball game without a team. Ensuring the ability for a search engine to crawl and index a website is, in large part, the focus for technical SEO.

What is a technical SEO audit? There's no standard definition commonly accepted by SEO professionals, but essentially, a technical SEO audit is an evaluation of a website as it interacts with search engine spiders or bots. Search engines get the information you see in the search results by operating software programs called *bots*, which follow links from page to page on the web, capturing content as they go. The content that search engine bots copy is organized into an index from which the search results process occurs. Okay, that's a simplification, but you should understand that search engines have to be able to copy your website content in order for it to appear in the search results. If there are difficulties or even inefficiencies with the process of a search engine bot doing its job, then it can mean web pages are not crawled and thus not included in the index or search results.

A technical SEO audit is one of several SEO audits typically conducted to determine the SEO readiness and effectiveness of a website. Research into keywords, content and on-page factors, links, and social signals, when combined with a technical SEO audit, provide a complete view of the opportunities for search engine success.

One mechanism for communicating ongoing technical SEO performance based on an audit is an SEO Scorecard. Scorecard reports are data rich or simplified according to who will be reading and using them in the organization. (See Figure 3.4. for a high-level SEO scorecard.)

There are plenty of books, blogs, and resources online focused on technical SEO and even information retrieval if you want to really dig into the topic. Ten years ago, Mike Grehan of Incisive Media wrote the first great book on SEO and how search engines work: *Search Engine Marketing: The Essential Best Practice Guide*. While there have been a near infinite number of changes since then, the book is still very relevant today. Two of the most useful resources are actually direct from the search engines themselves: Google's Webmaster Central and Bing's Webmaster Tools.[7, 8]

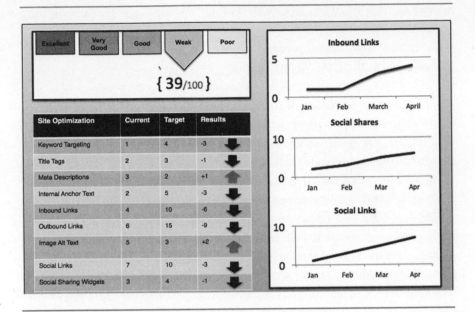

**FIGURE 3.4   SEO Audit Scorecard**

If you're a content marketing professional or a social media strategist, chances are pretty good that you won't be conducting a technical SEO audit yourself. However, there are some tools that can be quite helpful, such as those for doing research on keywords and links to the website in question. It's important to note that a tool's effectiveness is directly related to the abilities of the user, so it's important to have someone with experience and skills perform your technical SEO audit. Here are some of the tasks and tools that such an audit might include:

- Review current website search traffic and performance with Google Analytics or another analytics tool.
- Track inbound links with Majestic SEO or Open Site Explorer.
- Check the speed of pages with Google Page Speed Online.
- Review the content management system, templates, and source code.
- Check for duplicate, thin, or poor-quality content.
- Overview site SEO readiness from Alexa Site Audit.
- Document the site URL structure and map with Xenu Link Sleuth.

- Assess basic crawl issues with Google Webmaster Tools and Bing Webmaster Tools.
- Document keyword ranking with Advanced Web Ranking or Raven Tools (good for relative measures).

Collecting these pieces of information and conducting an analysis of the website from the perspective of how a search engine sees the content will help generate recommendations to improve the website's ability to attract organic search traffic. Current link, social, and search engine traffic analysis can reveal areas of opportunity for improvement as well as things that should be scaled up.

Links are like electricity for websites and are used by search engines to discover content as well as a factor in sorting or ranking content in search results. Evaluating link sources of your competitors that are already performing well in search can reveal new linking opportunities. That same link research can also show the quantity and quality of current links to your website, which serves as a baseline for where and how to improve.

The faster your pages load, the better the user experience for customers. It also means that Googlebot can crawl your website faster, and if you look at the billions of documents Google has to crawl, faster means more efficient for Google. That's why page speed has been made a signal to help determine page ranking.

Content management systems can be a source of many types of issues with a website's SEO performance. Templates that publish content from a database can be an SEO's friend or its worst nightmare depending on the ability to make changes. For example, dynamically populating title tags using reverse breadcrumb navigation can provide a strong, search-friendly feature to an entire website with a relatively small change to the templates and database. But if those changes aren't possible, a website could be stuck with a situation like uneditable title tags or the need to manually edit thousands of page titles.

Google has a preference for unique quality content, and efforts like the Google Panda Update have put more emphasis on content quality and uniqueness. If a website publishes slim content with more information in the navigation and footer than in the body of the page itself, those pages may not have a very good chance of appearing in the search results. If a website has a substantial amount of content that is deemed low-quality or duplicate content, then it can affect the entire website, even though the remaining pages are of high quality.

Basic SEO services like Alexa Site Audit provide a range of information that can be useful in assessing a websites search engine readiness and provide a prioritized list of recommendations. Xenu Link Slueth is free software that crawls your website and provides a report of all the URLs to help understand how the site is structured, to uncover any broken links, to check title tag length and redirects, and a host of other features. Microsoft offers a similar website SEO evaluation tool called Search Engine Optimization Toolkit.

Google and Bing Webmaster Tools provide another set of useful data about how their respective bots interact with your website. These webmaster dashboards provide information ranging from crawling errors to how often your site appeared and was clicked on to the number of inbound links. You also have the opportunity to indicate preferences about your website to the search engine, such as by submitting a site map or indicating a canonical URL or geographic target preference.

The value in a technical SEO audit for content marketers is that it helps remove any barriers to your valuable content from being included in search results and, in most cases, can improve the search visibility of your content significantly. When content marketing professionals ask why they should bother with SEO when their excellent content will be shared by the people who read it, I respond by pointing out that great content can be even greater if it's easy for interested readers to find and share. It's a competitive digital world, and for content publishers who want to maximize the availability of their content to people who are actively looking, then optimizing the keywords, content, code, social shares, and links of a website is essential.

The importance of good research on competitors, the search and social landscape, and a quality technical SEO audit cannot be understated. Capturing information about who your real competitors are in search can provide key observations about what keywords, media types, and promotion channels can be leveraged to gain the desired visibility on search engines. An understanding of social media conversations related to topics of interest to your brand, the competition, and how potential customers think of your products and services is also essential for developing an effective approach to social engagement. A technical SEO audit can provide marketers with a hit list of website and content management system improvements that will fix or improve the ability of search engines to crawl and index your content for availability in search engines. Additional technical SEO insight can provide opportunities to outsmart your competition by understanding the SEO tactics they're using and countering with an approach to your advantage.

So far, we've gained an understanding of where SEO and social media listening can assist our content marketing efforts for attracting and engaging customers. We've also dug into competitive and market research to identify the search and social landscape as well as steps to make sure our website is search engine–friendly. The next step in our planning phase of an optimized approach to content marketing is to identify the bigger picture of how an integrated approach to search and social media optimization will help achieve content and online marketing goals.

## ACTION ITEMS

1. Identify your online and real-world competitors. Are they the same?
2. When logged out of Google, research the types of content that appear in search results for your most important keywords. How does this match up with your content mix?
3. Conduct your own technical SEO audit using Alexa Site Audit, Majestic SEO, SpyFu Kombat, and SEOMoz tools. What are the most pressing opportunities?
4. Evaluate a few social media listening tools, such as Trackur, Radian6, or Vocus (TopRank client) to start capturing data about topics relevant to your business and your customers' interests.

# CHAPTER 4

## In It to Win It: Setting Objectives

It's pretty difficult to score if you don't have goals, yet many companies approach content and social media marketing as independent channels without clear business outcomes defined. Whether the goal is to acquire new customers and grow revenue or to facilitate public relations, recruiting, and customer service effectiveness, identifying tactical objectives and the steps to reach them is essential for success. This chapter covers setting goals specific to an SEO- and social media–focused content marketing strategy that seeks to increase traffic, leads, and sales as well as to improve media coverage, attract talented employees, and serve online customers more efficiently.

### THE ROLE OF SEARCH AND SOCIAL MEDIA WITH CONTENT MARKETING

Content is the basis for search and often an outcome of social media engagement. Joe Pulizzi of the Content Marketing Institute offers this definition: "Content marketing is a marketing technique of creating and distributing relevant and valuable content to attract, acquire, and engage a clearly defined and understood target audience—with the objective of driving profitable customer action."[1] Content marketing investments are often directed toward lead nurturing and prospect education with an ultimate goal to convert into a sale. As an independent tactic, content marketing goals can extend from key points in the buying cycle such as awareness and purchase to the entire customer life cycle, including customer support and advocacy.

Modern search engine optimization requires content and links, of course, but has increasingly relied on social signals as search engines factor the influence of authors, curators, and the rich data that can be found on the social web. The fundamental role of SEO is to help search engines find, copy, and understand a company's content as the best answer for the things their prospects and customers are looking for. SEO best practices can be applied to any kind of content that shows up in search results, whether it's a web page, image, video, PDF file, or a local business listing. While SEO is a perfect complement to content marketing and longer sales cycles, many investments in optimization are specifically to generate leads and sales, since search is an explicit expression of a need or want. If a person is ready to buy a product or service right now, he or she can find it through search and can make a purchase within a short amount of time. Most goals related to SEO start with key performance indicators like search visibility and keyword traffic that then lead to inquiries and sales.

Social media and networks are effective for information discovery, just as search engines are. Consumers often move between search and social channels for information that leads them to purchase, and this behavior presents a significant opportunity for companies to be wherever their customers are. Social networks can create awareness, build brand confidence, and influence purchase, referrals, and advocacy. Social media is also a platform for customer service interaction.

In her eMarketer report, Debra Aho Williamson states, "Integrating social media with other corporate activities is a key challenge for marketers, but incorporating it is the only way to be successful, long term."[2] On it's own, social media as a marketing channel can be hit or miss for many companies, because people don't tend to join social networks to make purchases. But integrating social media marketing and engagement with search, content marketing, e-mail, and other types of online marketing tactics can result in substantial benefits.

The diversity of business goals for social media investment is significant to the extent that a field called *social business* has evolved.[3] When you think of social media, it's usually in the context of companies invest-ing in external social media marketing and engagement with prospects and customers. However, companies are also looking inward for ways to use social technologies to foster collaboration, content, and exper-tise. That same collective intelligence used for knowledge transfer and collaboration internally can also be tapped for external marketing pur-poses. Companies like Intel, Best Buy, IBM, and Walmart are mobilizing employees to better use social communication channels internally and, in many cases, to connect with customers externally as well.[4, 5, 6, 7] Social media–related goals for a company will depend on the extent of the approach. Suffice it to say that business social media objectives also run the course of the entire customer life cycle, from creating awareness to influencing purchase to advocacy.

It's reasonable to have individual goals for investments in SEO, social media, and content marketing, but I think you can see that these disci-plines can work together to achieve an amplified effect on the ability for companies to attract, engage, and inspire customers to action. Now let's get into some specific goal setting relevant to different functions with in an organization that can best leverage a socialized and optimized con-tent strategy.

## IDENTIFYING ONLINE MARKETING OBJECTIVES

Before a business decides how, why, and what content to optimize and socialize, it's important to take a step back and ask this essential market-ing question, "What are we trying to do?" The answer is usually pretty obvious: "We're trying to get more people to buy what we're selling!"

That's the big picture for companies across the board, but practi-cal online marketing objectives will be unique to each company's indi-vidual situation. The role of content works across departments, and although we're talking specifically about marketing, the interaction between departmental content within a company can actually amplify overall business outcomes. When public relations works with market-ing, and marketing works with customer service, and recruiting works with public relations, there can be mutual benefit for each department as well as for the organization as a whole. Some companies want to increase their number of customers; some are more focused on revenue or profitability; others emphasize customer marketing and retention.

(See Figure 4.1.) These are all worthy business objectives, and from a content, search, and social media perspective, being able to tie marketing objectives to overall organizational goals is essential.

The mechanics of establishing marketing goals starts with a good understanding of current business performance and efforts to acquire and retain customers. Common areas of focus for an online marketing program that leverages SEO, social media, and content marketing include key performance indicators such as:

• Search visibility
• Social mentions
• Web page links
• Citations in traditional online media and blogs
• Social shares
• Social links
• Visitors to the company web
• Visitors to company social destinations
• Newsletter subscribers
• Blog and social content subscribers, fans, friends, and followers
• Comments and other measures of engagement

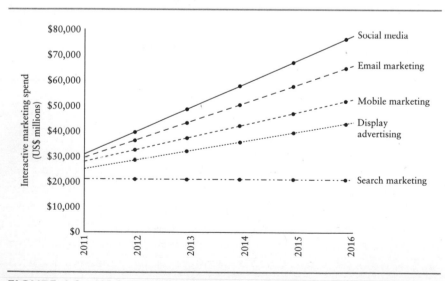

**FIGURE 4.1   US Interactive Marketing Spend**

Measurable marketing outcomes typically include:

- Fulfillment downloads
- Webinar or other online event participation
- Inquiries
- Leads
- Sales
- Referrals
- Brand advocacy

Having said all that, the simplest thing to do is assess your online marketing strategy for what has worked so far and what needs improvement. A review of your website analytics may show a steady increase in search traffic, yet there may be a significant opportunity to improve the quality of that traffic in terms of leads, sales, and profitability. For example, 10 visitors who spend an extended amount of time learning about your brand and your products are more valuable than 100 who bounce after a few seconds.

To tie marketing goals to overall business goals, think about how well the website is performing currently and what the overall online business goals are for the future. Look at each business goal, whether its focus is revenue, retention, or service, and then decide how that translates to content.

Business goals can be broad, but to create actionable plans to achieve your goals, break them down. For example, if you discovered leads that travel through your sales cycle fairly quickly are more apt to close, you'll want to decide what content marketing tactics you can put into place that will move leads faster through the lead-generation and nurturing process. If more leads close more quickly, your marketing objectives will be achieved more effectively. In this situation, you may want to target content optimization and promotion toward prospects that fit a fast-buyer profile.

Another example might involve creating a stronger sales message in your content by using resources that better educate and inform shoppers on issues that have slowed buyers in the past. Many efforts in social media marketing omit any effort toward the suggestion of a purchase. Although it's often a mistake to be *too* aggressive (or "salesy") on social networks, it's also a missed opportunity not to provide a way to continue the conversation in a business context if people want to do so.

For marketing-centric objectives, think about the specific things you want to accomplish through content that will ultimately lead to overall business goals, such as:

- Elevate brand perception
- Establish thought leadership
- Drive customer engagement
- Provide better customer service
- Increase customer retention
- Build a bigger referral network

Once there's a firm understanding of overall business goals, then you can map them to supporting marketing objectives.

Combining search and social media as channels to reach target markets means that content has to provide relevance according to where it's found and deliver specific problem-solving value based on what the target audience needs according to their position in the buying cycle. Searchers using broad keyword phrases may be focused on educational or informational-themed content to learn about the category of products and services. To serve those top-of-funnel information needs, our job as marketers is to create optimized content focused on answering those general questions. Content should be useful and compelling enough so that those who interact with it might be willing to share to their social networks. Part of social media optimization means making such sharing easy through the use of widgets that call out specific social networks like Facebook, LinkedIn, Twitter, and Google+.

Customers who are looking for your products and services specifically may be further along in the buying cycle, and therefore content needs to be created and optimized to address those specific information needs to guide the buyer to purchase.

Marketing-related goals for content that rely on search and social media for discovery must consider the overall business goals of the company, objectives that are specific to marketing, and the needs of the buyer whom you are after. Long-term business goals that are mapped to marketing will help keep the program in context of what's important to the business. An understanding of how to meet customer needs through content as inspiration to buy will achieve the win for all.


## ONLINE PUBLIC RELATIONS OBJECTIVES

Now that we have a good framework for defining online marketing objectives, we can explore how public relations objectives can be supported with our optimized and socialized content marketing strategy.

As with mapping organizational goals to marketing, it's also useful to associate overall business goals to public relations objectives. Think about how online PR can elevate brand awareness, build thought leadership, and inspire customer engagement and retention. Rather than being gatekeepers to stories and news, modern PR professionals are creators and curators of that news. It only makes sense to optimize news content for search demand and to encourage both social discovery and sharing.

Building relationships with influencers and the media, gaining media placements, occupying search results with positive brand content, inspiring brand awareness, and engagement all fall under common PR objectives that involve content. Combining SEO, social media, and content with PR goals means being able to craft and optimize stories that are in sync with search demand and social discovery by bloggers, journalists, analysts, and researchers as well as with customers. A report issued by the Arketi Group indicated that 95 percent of journalists use search engines.[8] A study by Cision and George Washington University reported that 89 percent of journalists use blogs and 65 percent use social networks for story research.[9] Customers are targets for marketers, so why can't the media be targets for PR using content optimization and social sharing? Making news content and subject matter experts easy to find for journalists can be a tremendous help for media relations efforts. At my agency, TopRank Online Marketing, we've gained anywhere from 5 to 20 unsolicited media placements per month without engaging a PR firm—all through news content that is easy to find in search and that is shared as popular content on social networks.

Facilitating social sharing of optimized stories will help increase awareness and further sharing among a community of interested participants. Today, every person is empowered to publish, so PR objectives related to optimized and socialized content marketing should consider more than just traditional online media, including the blogosphere and individual consumers who can tweet, update, comment, rate, and influence their own networks.

Your PR objectives should have at their root the same concept that drives search engine optimization success: a focus on the expectations of the audiences and how to serve as a valued resource for them.

The focus for most PR initiatives is to create awareness and influence, so imagine how you want your business to be perceived online. Establish objectives that all tie back to your original business goals with an underpinning of influence in mind. If you want to attract more customers and grow revenue, you should influence those who can help make that happen by making it easy for them to find your useful content though search and social media.

Of course, on the web, the currency of influence is content. So creating objectives that make news content more easily discoverable through search is a prime way to spread your influence. Analysts, journalists, and even some bloggers find newsrooms a useful resource for finding past media coverage, press releases, image assets, executive bios, company history, webinars, white papers, case studies, and other information helpful for researching stories. Content that lives in a newsroom can be optimized for better visibility both on search engines and for sharing on social networks.

Using online clipping services, web analytics, social media monitoring, and other social platform–specific measurement tools, the effect of optimizing and socializing PR content can be tracked and evaluated for better performance. If you're not currently tracking the SEO and social media impact on online PR, then base forecasting and goal setting in part on data from your current website analytics and blogging activity. Use the data you have to create a baseline of measurement for expected search and social media traffic. Set goals for key performance indicators (KPIs), such as mentions on blogs, social engagement with favorable brand mentions, and search referred traffic to your online newsroom. At the same time, estimate the impact those overall PR objectives could have on increasing search traffic through content like optimized press releases, images, video, social content, and other online news content. In many cases, you'll simply have to develop a hypothesis of what could happen based on whatever data is available to you and then implement social media and search optimization tactics to start collecting performance information. With actual data being collected, you can make refinements to optimization and social media tactics as well as to your forecast of the impact they're having.

## HR AND RECRUITING CONTENT OPTIMIZATION OBJECTIVES

Establishing marketing and public relations objectives represents the bulk of opportunity with optimized and socialized content. Buying products and writing news stories aren't the only reasons people search for information that companies provide. Another area of consumer and business communications to consider for optimization and social sharing is recruiting. Proper staffing is essential for companies of all sizes. The costs of finding, hiring, keeping—and even losing—an employee can be significant. Consider these statistics:[10]

- The total US market size for recruiting is approximately $124 billion.
- Talent acquisition spending rose 6 percent in 2011 over the year before.
- An average of $3,500 was spent on new hires, with most of that money going to search agencies and job boards.
- Large companies paid an average of $1,949 per hire.
- Small companies paid an average of $3,665 per hire.

It's clear that hiring is a lucrative business for companies that provide those services, but if you don't have the luxury or the money for staffing agencies or professional recruiters, you're most likely interested in keeping those costs down.

Enter the use of "socialize and optimize" in recruiting. The objectives you set for incorporating search and social might look like this: If your company is spending $10,000 per month on recruiting and talent acquisition costs (like job listings), then an objective of spending that same amount but with some efforts allocated to keyword-optimized job listings and social media promotion might carry a forecast of a 5 or 10 percent increase in qualified applicants.

To elaborate, say you're an investment firm with an institutional sales job opening in Austin, Texas, looking to accomplish this objective. In addition to the regular job boards and advertisements you use to spread word about your latest job openings, you can optimize your job description for location as well as company or skill set. Leveraging that optimized content on search engines will help those perfect potential employees find and connect with you, potentially reducing your need to engage with job aggregator services.

Another example might involve a desire to improve the quality of candidates you find so you can limit the training costs associated with new employees. You might create an objective to target 15 more highly qualified candidates per month who more closely match the sophisticated job skills your technical positions require. This could lead to efforts of finding more "silent candidates" (i.e., those who aren't actively seeking a new job but who would be perfect for what you need). While those candidates might not be looking, their social networks might pass along the job opportunity.

By separating objectives according to the situation, such as creating a cost savings of a certain percent or a decreased investment in outside recruitment services by a certain percent, you can then plan for and create the appropriate optimized content marketing tactics that will help you reach those goals.

## CUSTOMER SERVICE OBJECTIVES

By now, your optimization objectives are firing on all cylinders. You've created a stream of search- and social media–friendly content that's relevant for attracting new customers and great visibility in the media. The best new candidates in the country are finding your job openings, and your business is humming along. But wait, it could get even better. You could add even more value to your business with another audience: your current customers.

Optimizing and socializing content meant for existing customers is not usually on the radar for companies that invest in SEO or social media marketing. However, consider these example goals:

- Reduce customer service hours by 10 percent, providing a reduced expenditure of $20,000.

- Increase online customer care visits by 20 percent, thereby reducing calls to the customer service center by 10 percent.

These objectives can be met by making your customer service information easier to find through both search and social media, keeping in mind that these audiences are looking for information after they've already purchased your products or services. There's tremendous benefit in keeping customers happy and satisfied with your customer service. Optimizing knowledge base, frequently asked questions, or public customer support content might be a golden opportunity to do just that.

For example, let's say you manufacture and sell universal remote controls. There are numerous products on the market and most all of them aren't what many people would consider user-friendly. The types of calls into your call center may be time- and cash-consuming. Imagine that an eight-minute call costs $32.50 in personnel and technology costs. Perhaps on average you receive 300 calls per day asking four common questions.

Now imagine that you've done a little homework to identify that there's a notable amount of search activity for support information about those products, and you either optimize or create and optimize an online help center to address those common problems. Taking the burden off of your customer service center saves time and money, and, in addition, you've created goodwill and trust by solving problems present in all remotes—not just yours.

At the end of the day, whether you set marketing, public relations, customer service, or recruiting objectives, all must be accountable to your overall business goals. KPIs and success metrics comprise more than just collecting data. They involve the application of careful analytics to understand progress toward your goals. Whether it's search or social media channels that drive traffic to your content, you'll be able to identify both channel-specific and overall goals to help your business become more successful.

We get into the nuts and bolts of measurement and analytics in Chapter 14, but in the meantime, let's get on to the next step in your journey toward an "optimized" state of mind—creating a content marketing strategy and road map.

## ACTION ITEMS

1. What are your overall online marketing goals?
2. What online public relations goals could you affect with optimized content?
3. When you place your next job listing, consider keywords in the job title, description, and link text.
4. Find out the most common customer service questions and develop a content plan to create and optimize that content online.

# CHAPTER 5

## Roadmap to Success: Content Marketing Strategy

A house is only as stable as its foundation, and so far we've covered several foundational concepts for an effective content marketing strategy, from understanding where search engine optimization, social media, and content intersect to essential research and customer-persona development. Translating these key pieces of the puzzle will help you take one of the most important steps in the journey to an optimized content marketing strategy.

In this chapter we will cover both the independent roles of search optimization, social media, and content marketing and a framework for integrating an approach that can improve overall online marketing effectiveness.

From my long-time experience working in sales, SEO, and web development, I've encountered a wide variety of business marketing problems and observed some common threads. In this chapter I will discuss common issues faced by content marketers and how a more holistic approach to integrated search, social media, and content marketing can result in improved marketing performance, more sales, and better customer experiences.

## INHERITING AN ONLINE MARKETING MESS

When Don Glass assumed his new role as director of marketing at a five-year-old software company, he inherited the marketing legacy of his predecessor. This included siloed marketing and advertising tactics, an out-of-date website, long-expired SEO efforts, a token social media presence, and heavy pay-per-click (PPC) advertising expenses. Efforts were almost exclusively focused on customer acquisition and very little ongoing communication with customers outside of solving customer service issues. There was even less outside communication with industry thought leaders or the media.

For this software company, leads were primarily sourced from word of mouth, online advertising, and trade shows, but quality and quantity were on a steady decline as competition increased and more companies in the space became involved with awareness and branding efforts through social networking, content marketing, and industry media coverage.

With minimal resources, Don Glass was tasked with (1) developing an online marketing strategy that would lift marketplace awareness of his software company as the most relevant in the category and (2) increasing the quantity and quality of leads while reducing online advertising costs.

Sound familiar? Maybe your situation isn't so bad. Or maybe it's worse.

One of the first steps Don Glass had to take was to gain a clear understanding of overall business objectives in terms of position in the marketplace, revenue growth, customer relationships, and future expansion or changes within the product mix. As we discussed in the previous chapter, identifying overall business goals helps you understand what impact marketing can have across the organization. There's an obvious connection between marketing, leads, and sales for revenue growth. But there's also a potential impact that marketing can have on other business objectives, such as building thought leadership and media attention, attracting talent, and fostering better relationships with customers for retention and referral goals.

Don's challenge was a formidable one, but by approaching it holistically and from a customer perspective, we'll see how the intersection of content, search, and social will prove a significant way to attract customers, engage them, and inspire them to buy as well as to share. Let's start to unravel the solution for Don and maybe your own by better understanding the role of content marketing.

## WHY YOUR BUSINESS NEEDS A CONTENT MARKETING STRATEGY

Not only is every brand a potential publisher, but so are consumers. The ability for anyone to create and share online has resulted in a growing wave of content. According to comScore, Google.com handles more than 11 billion searches each month.[1] YouTube serves up 3 billion videos each day.[2] Facebook now has more than 800 million active users.[3] Twitter is publishing more than 200 million tweets per day.[4] LinkedIn has more than 100 million users, FourSquare grew 3,400 percent in 2010, and Pinterest has reached more than 11 million unique monthly visitors.[5,6,7] Consumers are active participants in the content creation and consumption universe. Brands that watch from the sidelines with a wait-and-see approach may find themselves joining in with too little, too late in a never-ending game of catch-up.

The variety of options for customer marketing and engagement, ranging from social media to SEO to e-mail marketing to online advertising, can be overwhelming. As a result, some of the most common online marketing questions I hear from client-side marketers revolve around, "How do we decide which online marketing tactics are best?"

Answering that question starts with a clear understanding of goals, customers, and a flexible online marketing strategy that assembles the right mix of tactics and measurement practices. Most companies are looking to acquire more customers and to retain those they have, but the question is, "How do we acquire and engage customers more efficiently and effectively?"

Consumers are not interested in interruption marketing. They want to be educated and entertained, and they increasingly expect value of some kind from brands before ever getting into a purchase situation. Both B2B and B2C customers expect to find answers as well as the products and services they're looking for via search engines. They also expect to interact socially with what they find on search engines. In fact, Google is making social connections possible without ever leaving the search results page by allowing logged-in Google users to add authors of content to their Google+ circles. (See Figure 5.1.)

Consumers expect content from brands. They also expect ease of discovery as well as the ability to interact with and socially share content with others who have similar interests. These aren't "nice to haves" anymore—they're expected.

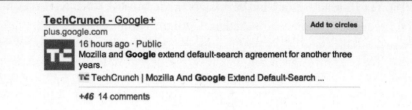

**FIGURE 5.1    Author Avatars and Instant Add to Circles on Google**

Most corporate marketing is structured to create content around products and services versus a publisher approach that emphasizes audience interests. As a result, the idea of implementing a content marketing program can seem foreign. However, the abundance of publishing tools and platforms now makes it possible for companies to create content and media that rivals some news organizations. A few great examples of highly influential and robust content marketing initiatives created by brands include OPEN Forum by American Express, Tablespoon.com by General Mills, and the Radian6 series of e-books, videos, blogs, and white papers.

Content fuels customer engagement at all stages of the customer life cycle, from the top of the funnel to advocacy. Content can educate prospects about your products and services, and it can also help educate about the buying process and how to get the most out of the purchase. Content can continue to reinforce the brand and customer relationship and inspire renewals, upgrades, and referrals.

The challenge is for companies to rethink their content marketing strategy and incorporate social media and SEO in order to fulfill customer expectations for ease of discovery, consumption, and sharing. On top of that, content must educate and make it easy to follow a logical conclusion to buy. The companies that do those things best will win it for themselves and for their customers.

## A HOLISTIC APPROACH TO CONTENT MARKETING

Understanding relationships between disparate channels can be new territory for many marketers. My favorite food metaphor for the relationship between search, social, and content is a peanut butter and jelly sandwich, with SEO as the peanut butter, social media as the jelly, and content as the bread that holds it all together. Content is the reason search engines exist, and although it's a simple concept, keep in mind that the primary value provided by search engines is to connect people with answers, and this fact shouldn't be lost in the sea of tactics, tricks, and pontification that goes on in the digital marketing world.

An optimized content marketing strategy is a plan for delivering thoughtful content with certain audiences and outcomes in mind. In the context of a company working to achieve its goals by being useful to its customers, community, and constituents, content isn't just king, it's the *kingdom*.

In the past, many companies have viewed content as a one-time effort for use with a company website, and they have often viewed content as too difficult to commit to when it came to blogging, articles, or media creation. However, that view has changed. According to a 2012 report, Content Marketing Institute found that 9 out of 10 organizations market with content, and 60 percent of respondents to the survey reported an intention to increase spending on content marketing within the next 12 months.

## Six Steps for a Better Content Marketing Strategy

1. *Objectives*. Identify your overall business goals for content marketing, including end goals such as an increase in leads and sales, media coverage or recruiting to key performance indicators (KPIs) such as increased search traffic, and social engagement. We discussed this in detail throughout Chapter 4, and the importance of identifying goals transcends any particular marketing channel, as you will see in the rest of the book.
2. *Audience*. Research customer segments and develop profiles that represent consistent characteristics, such as pain points, motivators to purchase, and social engagement. To find out how personas fit within an "optimize and socialize" content marketing strategy, be sure to read Chapter 6.
3. *Content plan*. An understanding of customer needs and business goals can be translated into a specific content plan that identifies relevant content mix, topics, and desired outcomes as they apply across the customer buying cycle. Chapter 8 gets into the nitty-gritty of how to develop a content plan.
4. *Promotion*. In concert with content planning, creation, and optimization is the planned promotion of content to end users as well as

to influencers for further sharing that will expose brand messages to new and relevant audiences. One of the fringe benefits of promoting useful content are links, and we discuss specific tactics for promotion in Chapter 12.

5. *Engagement.* Growing social networks and community through listening, participation, and content sharing provides insight for future content, enables advocacy, and reinforces sharing behaviors. How do you grow your network and increase engagement? Look for details in Chapter 11.

6. *Measurement.* Are our content marketing efforts helping customers? Are those interactions leading to intended behaviors such as inquiries, sharing, and sales? How are our broader business goals aided through content marketing efforts? What are the KPIs telling us about individual and collective tactics? Capture insight and refine future content marketing efforts accordingly. You get answers to these questions and more in Chapter 13.

Armed with good reasons for using a content marketing strategy and a framework for building an effective one, we can move on to the role of SEO in attracting prospects and buyers to our content through relevant visibility on search engines.

## SEARCH ENGINE OPTIMIZATION STRATEGY

If Google were dating the SEO community, the Facebook status would read: "It's complicated." Both Google and Bing have made substantial efforts to create resources for the webmaster community, starting with Vanessa Fox and Google Webmaster Tools. Bing has its own version of webmaster resources that helps website owners gain insight into how each search engines interact with websites so problems can be identified and the process of getting a website crawled and indexed is as efficient as possible. These tools from search engines for website owners provide a valuable feedback mechanism that they can use to advance performance in hopes of better visibility for customers that are looking.

The complication comes into play with the rapid rate of change and decisions like Google's choice to encrypt keyword-referring data from search traffic that comes from users logged into Google. The impact of this approach on ensuring privacy for users has been estimated to be in the single digits to low double digits of all organic search traffic. Without knowing which keywords drive traffic to their web pages, webmasters are at a disadvantage about how to optimize those pages for better user experience and marketing performance, let alone search visibility. Search engines like Google and Bing are continuously testing and making improvements and rolling out new features on their search engines. In 2010 alone, Google ran more than 6,000 experiments.

An effective SEO strategy should involve several different audits as well as ongoing work to implement best practices, refine results, and take advantage of trending opportunities. I liken content marketing without significant keyword and optimization consideration to "hiding" your content. Search represents a substantial opportunity for prospects, customers, potential employees, and the media to discover your content. Why not make it easier and more effective for an audience that is actively looking to find your brand's information online?

Traditionally, SEO has worked independently of other marketing tactics, but that's not the world we live in today. Instead of bringing SEO expertise in after content has been created, keyword research should be initiated at the time of creating the content plan. Customer segmentation and persona data can contribute significantly to how effective content optimization aligns with customer needs. Understanding what customers care about relevant to your product and services mix can elevate the relevance of the searcher user experience, thus resulting in more click-throughs, time on site, and sales.

A baseline understanding of a company's current search performance compared to overall revenue goals will help identify projections for what SEO can contribute to a content marketing strategy. The particulars involve knowledge about the competitive marketplace, customer needs, and resources the company has available related to content, networking, analytics, and ongoing promotions.

## HOW SEO CAN WORK WITH CONTENT STRATEGY

Organizations can advance their reach and engagement goals through content marketing, and it's the content strategist's role to audit, develop strategy, plan, create, and maintain that content. Ahava Leibtag provided a practical approach to creating content with purpose in her post,

"Creating Valuable Content," on the Content Marketing Institute site, which outlines how content should be findable, readable, understandable, actionable, and shareable.

SEO and content strategy intersect in more ways than optimizing web pages with keywords. Answering the question, "How does SEO and content strategy interact?" starts with understanding customer segments, behaviors, and preferences for information discovery, consumption, and sharing. Knowing what customers care about and how those concerns and interests manifest as search keywords and social topics folds very well into the keyword research practiced by professional SEOs.

Keyword glossaries and editorial plans aid in planning relevant content that is inherently optimized for customers and target audiences. Specific keyword optimization is appropriate as well, but the end content product becomes much easier to find, consume, and share if there's empathy with customer needs translated into topics and keywords from the start. I'm a fan of optimizing for customers before search engines, but you can certainly do both.

An editorial plan outlines content types, topics, and the keywords they're optimized for. It indicates where and whether the content will be republished and repurposed. The plan also shares which channels of distribution will be used to promote the content and share it via the social web. Search engine optimization also applies to social media content that emphasizes popular and relevant social topics versus search keywords.

Planning, creating, optimizing, promoting, and engaging with content on topics that customers and target audiences care about is where modern SEO has evolved: content marketing optimization. SEO expertise, which also includes knowledge of how search engines crawl and index websites, content management systems, and the impact of how websites are coded and organized, provides a powerful ally to content strategists when goals and objectives are in alignment.

## FIVE ESSENTIAL SEO AUDITS

In Chapter 3 we discussed the internal research task of a technical SEO audit. In order to maximize the impact of natural search visibility, there's more for us to consider beyond website code and search engine bots crawling web pages. To the extent that SEO would contribute to the achievement of key marketing goals, here's a breakdown of the five audits that will assess a baseline:

1. *Keyword research*. Customers often speak a different language when it comes to search, so it's important to identify what phrases represent the mix of reasons for using Google or Bing to find solutions like those offered by your company. People search for many reasons other than to buy products and services, so keyword research can provide essential insight into the demand for topics relevant to any area of your website, from jobs to news to customer support. A keyword research audit will assess your website, competitors, consumers, web analytics, and keyword research tools to identify, organize, and manage your target search keyword phrases. Chapter 7 digs into the finer art and science of discovering which keywords will best motivate customer actions like leads and sales.

2. *Content audit*. Once target keyword phrases have been identified, a comparison with current website content is made to determine optimization opportunities as well as to recommend new content creation. A website must be the best resource for a topic, and content optimization takes inventory of all content and digital assets that could be a potential entry point via search and recommends SEO copywriting tactics to showcase those pages as most relevant. Chapters 9 and 10 dig deeper into the role of original content, curated content, and the specifics of on-page optimization.

3. *Technical SEO audit*. If search engines have difficulty finding, crawling, and indexing your content, it may put your site at a disadvantage. Search engines are far from perfect, so the more website owners and marketers can do to help the engines do their job, the more advantage you can create for desired visibility in search.

4. *Link footprint*. Links help search engines and customers alike find your content. Links from one page to another, or those shared on social platforms, serve as a signal that can be factored by search engines as they decide the best answers to display in the search results. A link footprint audit identifies the quantity and quality of links from web and social sources pointing to your content. A comparison with top-performing websites in your industry and keyword category can reveal numerous opportunities. We explore those tactics in Chapter 12.

5. *Social SEO audit*. The influence of social media on search engine visibility has increased substantially in recent years. Assessing a brand's

social presence, engagement, and distribution through social channels is as much an audit with SEO implications as it is for social media marketing. Understanding a brand's social authority and content distribution can lead to a much improved approach, with benefits to customers as well as to the business.

We dig into several of these SEO audits more specifically in the implementation phase. If there's a market demand through search for solutions offered by a company, then SEO is essential for maximizing that opportunity. For companies that expect to gain new business, protect their online reputation, grow social networks, attract new employees, and provide a great user experience with online customer support, then SEO is imperative.

## SOCIAL MEDIA MARKETING STRATEGY

Most practitioners in the social media space talk about developing a strategy specifically for social media. They describe the importance of social media listening with a monitoring tool, setting up a presence on platforms like Facebook, Twitter, and YouTube, and having a company blog. There's another school of thought that says social media strategy isn't what companies need, but rather a marketing strategy that factors in social media where it matters.

This may seem like a matter of semantics, but it makes a big difference organizationally, logistically, and especially with implementation and measurement. Social media marketing is new to many companies, and therefore they often place it in the realm of public relations or marketing. The reality is that social media participation runs across an entire organization.

Should a company have a point of view toward the organization's approach to social media participation? Of course. Most social media policies provide guidelines for employees as well as the company's vision for where social participation, media creation, sharing, and engagement fit within the overall business strategy. As companies mature their social media marketing efforts, they may find social participation and collaboration benefits that compel investments beyond social media marketing into social business.

While some marketing thought leaders like Guy Kawasaki have suggested that you don't need a social media strategy, others like Chris Brogan say you do. Whether you approach your brand's social web participation purely as a reaction and adaptation based on how social channels interact with your social content or you're able to consider specific audiences and tactics with a plan to achieve certain goals, there's no mistaking that consumers expect brand involvement on the social web. The challenge is deciding which approach will work best for your company.

As with our strategies for content marketing and search engine optimization, an effective approach to social media marketing follows a similar path:

- *Objectives.* Social media is more than marketing, so consider not only the ability to create more brand awareness, thought leadership, and influence on sales, but also the role of social media tools for any kind of external communications.

- *Listening.* Establishing a social media monitoring effort is essential for data capture that will reveal where conversations are happening about topics relevant to customers and your business goals. Listening is as important as web analytics for ongoing involvement in social channels.

- *Audience.* Are your customers active on the social web, and where? What do they do? What do they talk about? Who are the influencers for topics of relevance to your business? What has your customer research revealed in terms of social participation, behaviors for content discovery, consumption, and sharing for target audiences? The process of understanding what customers want in exchange for their attention is ongoing.

- *Participation and content.* As you come to understand where your target audience of buyers and influencers spend their time, you'll also see where to establish a presence, share useful content, and engage the community. It's tempting to focus on Facebook, Google+, blogging, and Twitter, but make an effort to grow beyond the popular social crowd into niche areas that have less noise and more influence according to your understanding of customers. Allocate some time to experimental channels, as well, to show your willingness to be innovative and to plant seeds in growing communities.

- *Measurement.* From key performance indicators such as fans, friends, and comments to business outcomes like network growth, engagement, and sales, measurement is essential for effective brand social media participation. Ongoing listening using social media monitoring tools ranging from Trackur to Radian6 will be important to measure the impact on conversations of your social content. Social media marketing management tools like Awareness, Vitrue, and Hootsuite will help manage and measure social content promotion. Web analytics tools like Google Analytics will provide insight into the social media–sourced traffic and engagement that occurs on your website.

## TYING IT ALL TOGETHER: AN OPTIMIZED AND SOCIALIZED CONTENT MARKETING STRATEGY

The marketing mess that Don Glass inherited (described at the beginning of this chapter) was ripe for an "optimize and socialize" approach. A content marketing strategy that considers audience, competitive landscape, and business goals, along with a supporting mix of search and social media tactics, is an instrumental approach for increasing awareness, boosting sales, and inspiring more customer engagement and sharing.

Think about your business goals in the context of a holistic content marketing approach. What would be the impact on your business of improved content discovery, consumption, and sharing among a community of customers and industry influencers? What do you know about your customers that can translate into search keywords and social topic insight? How do content, distribution channels, search visibility, and social engagement factor into your overall approach to attract, engage, and inspire customers to buy?

## ACTION ITEMS

1. What are the most important online marketing objectives for your business?
2. Besides marketing, where in your organization's content creation efforts could you apply an "optimize and socialize" approach?
3. Identify the listening, research, and analytics tools you'll use to benchmark your search and social media program performance.
4. Develop an integrated content, SEO, and social media strategy that employs the goal-setting, competitive, and customer research ideas outlined in Chapters 2 to 4.

# PHASE 2

# IMPLEMENTATION

# CHAPTER 6

## Know Thy Customer: Personas

The first phase of our journey toward an optimized state of mind focused on planning and we covered a lot of important ground from the applications of social media optimization and content marketing for small, large, B2B, and B2C companies to the principles of content discovery, consumption, and engagement. With a holistic approach in mind, we discussed business objectives and strategies for integrated search engine optimization, social media, and content marketing. It's a lot of groundwork, but there's merit to the saying "He who fails to plan, plans to fail" (anonymous) that makes it worthwhile. In phase two, "implementation," we'll put that planning into action, starting with personas.

### THE WHAT AND WHY OF CUSTOMER PERSONAS

Demystifying better search, social media, and content marketing often starts with doing a better job of connecting with customers in more relevant ways. But how can you connect with customers if you don't know who they are or what they care about? Most SEO efforts are focused on creating and optimizing content against a list of keywords. But keywords don't buy products and services—customers do. To really make a difference with more effective online marketing, businesses should become more sophisticated in their understanding of customer needs, behaviors, and preferences. That means optimizing for customers and outcomes by researching and segmenting customer data to develop customer personas.

So, what is a persona? According to *The Buyer Persona Manifesto*, a *persona* is "an archetype, composite picture of the real people who buy, or might buy, products like the ones you sell."[1] Developed in the mid-1990s by Angus Jenkinson, the notion of personas is based on a representation of collective prospect and buyer characteristics that can draw from a wide range of data sources and types, including demographic and behavioral, as well as preferences for content discovery, consumption, and engagement. Working with personas is an act of empathizing with customer needs and organizing common sets of characteristics into a corresponding profile. Insight into customer needs will help you develop a more relevant and effective content marketing approach.

For example, "Bill Engineer" might represent a 35-year-old man who is married with children and owns his own home. He has worked in mechanical engineering for 10 years and travels about six times per year. He owns an iPad, a smart phone, and several computers at home. He connects to news, entertainment, and friends digitally, but rarely uses social media channels for professional sharing. Bill's preferred search engine is Google. He rarely clicks on ads (but does so occasionally when one is relevant), and he uses Google Reader to subscribe to online news. He's busy and doesn't spend much time on any social network other than Facebook and LinkedIn, and when he does, it's usually via his iPad. He consumes social and online news content daily, but briefly, early in the morning and in the evenings. His content preferences include sports, technology, games, electronics/gadgets, cars, and Maker Faire projects. Bill is always interested in finding ways, even it costs him a little more, to simplify, automate, and carve out more time to spend with his family.

Based on what we know about Bill Engineer, we can make some preliminary decisions about content and topics relevant to a brand's products and services. We want to understand where Bill is coming from and what he cares about. The context for how he discovers information, the topics and format of that content, and what motivates him to engage or buy are essential for connecting with the persona of Bill Engineer in a meaningful way.

By knowing what a customer group cares about, marketers can do a better job of creating relevant content that is easy to find on search engines and social media websites that inspires them to buy and share. Information gleaned from developing personas can inspire all aspects of content marketing and optimization, including keyword research, editorial plans, social networking, and promotion.

## WHY CUSTOMER SEGMENTS AND PERSONAS ARE IMPORTANT

With the study of customer data collected online, customer segments can be created and named. The testing of various products, services, and price points allows different offers to be made to different segments, often with great accuracy. However, when the data is taken a step further, it can do more than answer the question, "What can we sell them next?" It can be used to assemble personas. As we build these personas, they can take on shape in our minds, just as brick-and-mortar retail merchants learn to distinguish between the sampler and the buyer, the economy-minded customers and the spendthrifts.

Persona development goes beyond simply selling more right now or favoring spendthrifts over economical customers. When customers become "real" in our minds (e.g., Bill Engineer), we can listen to them and learn what they really care about. Understanding your customer groups in this way helps us gain a sense of how they like to find and engage with online content. The better the alignment of content availability and relevance with customer interests, the more effective our content marketing efforts become at increasing sales and customer satisfaction.

A marketing focus on personas can also help assemble a more targeted and effective content plan. The ease of publishing and distributing content on the Internet has motivated many marketers to take a shotgun approach to copywriting and SEO. Such tactics focus on lists of the most popular keywords to be used as inspiration to create new content in the hope it will lead to conversions. While a gross increase in optimized content may lead to some sales, it can also create websites that are large and hard to manage, as well as a body of content that is more mechanical than meaningful to customers. Google, in particular, frowns on lower-quality content through the application of processes and updates like Panda, which can affect a website's ranking if a substantial number of pages are deemed low quality. Persona-guided content is more relevant and useful, thereby appealing both to search engines and customers. The answer isn't just quality, it's the quantity of quality content that is relevant and easy to find that inspires readers to act.

Understanding the persona takes online marketing segmentation to the next level by focusing less on corporate egocentrism of promoting products, hoping someone will buy, and more on understanding what motivates customers to want to buy.

## A PROCESS FOR DEVELOPING BUYER PERSONAS

Creating buyer personas as part of your content, search, and social media marketing strategy involves a range of activities intended to reveal groups of customers with common characteristics whom you can associate with a common identity. With a clear understanding of your overall business goals as discussed in Chapter 4, the information and analysis of customer personas will be instrumental in formulating your editorial plan, keywords, social content, and promotion tactics. The fundamental steps for persona development are shown in Figure 6.1.

1. *Identify key customer attributes.* There are ideal customers and there are customers to be avoided. Write down some of the high-level characteristics of your best customers. What motivates them? What do they care about? What are their goals and behaviors? Do the same for your worst customers and two or three other categories of customers that come to mind.
2. *Collect data.* In addition to demographic information, some of the data points to collect include job title and time in current position, nature of work and responsibilities, job dissatisfaction, any concerns, needs, and interests relevant to brand solutions, role in buying process, where they fit in the buying cycle, motivators, social media preferences, search preferences, website interactions, buying and product preferences, and methods of online information access.

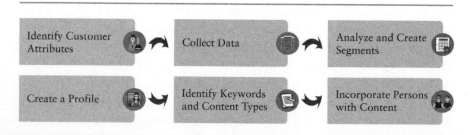

**FIGURE 6.1   Steps toward Persona Development and Implementation with Content Marketing**
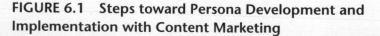

These data points can be compiled into a template for reuse. We'll cover data collection in more detail later in this chapter.

3. *Analyze and create segments.* Analysis of the data collected will reveal patterns, trends, and common characteristics. Correlations between data points can provide key differentiators between segments. Do customers who convert to sales from social channels hold different jobs and influence in purchase decisions than those who buy from search or e-mail? Are motivations for purchase distinctly different with types of job roles, time in position, or even interests? Compare the ideal customer characterizations and the worst with the data you've collected. Draw some conclusions from the patterns that emerge about specific traits.

4. *Create a profile for target audiences.* Depending on the company, mix of products and services, and variations within the customer base, anywhere from 3 to 10 or more personas are created. A profile for each persona should include the essential data points necessary to understand the context and motivations for that customer group relevant to your business goals. It's a common practice to give your customer profile a name, as we did earlier in the chapter for Bill Engineer. References to this name in your marketing plans will help create consistency in how you implement and measure the impact of a particular persona on your content marketing, optimization, and social media engagement efforts.

5. *Identify keyword groups and content types for personas.* As we come to understand what motivates different personas, the topics they're interested in, and how they use search and social media to discover information online, we can extract topics. Those topics of focus can be distilled into groups of keywords. Topics also inspire the content plan that meets the information needs of the prospects as they move through the buying cycle. Some personas will be attracted to distinctly different topics, and other categories will be a matter of nuance and slight refinement. Persona-guided content, optimization, and social engagement should facilitate more-relevant experiences with brand content, shortening time to sale, improving satisfaction, and increasing the likelihood of sharing and referral.

6. *Incorporate with content creation, optimization, and promotion.* The key pain points and motivations of your personas should be aligned with a buying cycle. Plan your content topics to address those needs and concerns so they inspire confidence and support your customers' motivation to buy. Understanding what the buyers

are trying to accomplish and providing content to aid in their journey for mutual benefit is essential for an effective content marketing optimization strategy. Content topics, keyword optimization, and social promotion should work in concert with the stages of the buying cycle and needs of the persona in question. Persona insights will then guide which topics are promoted through optimization as well as social media channels.

## COLLECTING DATA FOR PERSONAS

Now that you have an idea of the process for constructing personas, we can dig a little deeper into how to collect the initial data. (See Figure 6.2.) A large portion of the data for your persona development effort will include demographics information and insights from web analytics. Some of the most valuable information will come from surveys and interviews. It's important to strike a quantitative and qualitative balance. Here are some examples of data sources you might use:

- Surveys of existing customers, prospects, and frontline employees
- Web analytics and conversion data

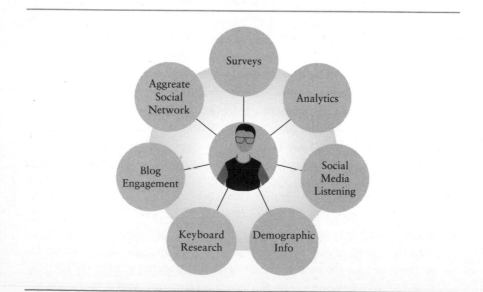

**FIGURE 6.2    Data Collection for Persona Development**

- Social media listening and monitoring tools
- Demographic information from Alexa, Quantcast, or DoubleClick Ad Planner
- Keyword research using Google AdWords Keyword Tool, Ubersuggest, SEMRush
- Blog engagement information from PostRank
- Aggregate user information from services like Fliptop

The data you collect can be compiled and analyzed to reveal common characteristics for persona development. Personas can then guide editorial direction for landing pages, blogs, social media content, and company web pages. Marketers and content creators who read a persona description must come away feeling like they've met someone real.

## HOW PERSONAS GUIDE CONTENT CREATION AND OPTIMIZATION

As you accumulate information about your customers, you'll want to identify common characteristics and patterns. Those behaviors that contribute to your business objectives, such as sales, advocacy, sharing, referrals, and repeat business, might fall into an "ideal" customer persona. That means there's another end to the spectrum—patterns that reflect undesirable customer behaviors, which might be associated with an "avoid" persona. There are several types of personas in between, according to where they fall in line with your company's business goals.

Understanding the pain points, goals, and topical preferences of customer personas provides invaluable insight into planning content to guide those customers through the buying cycle. The motivations and context that bring customers to search or tap into their social networks for recommendations can be translated into tactics. (See Figure 6.3.)

- *Content plan.* Based on the need, pain point, or goal for your ideal customer persona, identify whether content already exists to meet it. If sufficient content does not exist, incorporate it into the content plan for creation. Map your customer needs (e.g., "How can I back up my computer without having to worry about losing disks or remembering to schedule?") to specific content such as an article,

| Situation | Your company sells a series of time saving & scheduling applications for smart phones. |
|---|---|
| Goals | • Increase product awareness<br>• Grow networks<br>• Increase citations in media & social<br>• Increase sales |
| Persona Overview  | **Name: Joe Small Business Owner**<br>**Title: CEO**<br>**Industry: B2B Software Sales**<br><br>**Pain Points**<br>• Minimal Budget<br>• Would like an assistant but cannot afford costs<br>• Works 60-80 hours per week<br>• Has trouble managing his calendar for meetings and other obligations |
| Brand Solution | • SEO<br>• Content Planning<br>• Social Media Strategy |
| Search Keywords | • Virtual Assistant<br>• Apps for phone<br>• Help Me Organize |
| Social Topics | • Time saving tips for business owners<br>• Get organized in 10 minutes a day<br>• Time is Money: Tips on increasing efficiencies at a minimal cost |

**FIGURE 6.3    Example Persona**

a how-to video, or even a product page that will help guide that persona along in the sales cycle.

- *SEO and Keywords.* Search phrases in demand that represent the product or service relevant to the persona's need should be researched for popularity and competitiveness. Based on the preceding backup example, do research beyond the obvious "computer backup," including phrases that describe situations or scenarios such as "computer backup without disks" or "automatic computer backups." Keyword-optimize existing content and incorporate SEO copywriting into the task list for ongoing creation of content according to the content plan. We will cover more on keyword research in Chapter 7.

- *Social media presence and participation.* In which social channels do specific customer personas participate? Where are they influenced?

Based on persona social media participation, determine whether a brand presence exists at all. If so, does it share and engage with content related to the ideal customer persona's needs and goals? If not, factor that social content opportunity into the brand social media strategy for creating a social presence. What social topics is the persona motivated by? Do threads of discussion already exist in social channels relevant to the customer goals? How can your brand be an authoritative voice on those topics? Incorporate relevant social topics in your community management, social content, and engagement approach relevant to the ideal customer persona.

In the assessment of existing web page and social assets, determine how well those search and social media assets perform in terms of ranking and social visibility. Reconcile the difference between current performance and the ideal in order to better attract, engage, and inspire the target persona. Add new content, optimization, and social engagement tasks accordingly. Also consider which metrics will help you identify successful efforts to connect with your ideal persona.

A fragmented effort within search, social media, and content marketing helps no one—not customers, and certainly not companies. Competition for attention within search results and on the social web is only going to increase as more brands become publishers and more customers create and socially share content. The need to create a relevant experience for your target customers in an online world of information overload is more important now than ever. Smart marketers would do well for themselves and the customers they're trying to reach by investing in the development of personas that reflect the desires, goals, and key traits of their best customers. Translating customer insight into quality keyword optimization of web pages, social content, and digital assets for specific phrases according to the searcher's needs in the buying cycle is an important step, along with social engagement. As a result, you'll deliver a more relevant experience for both search engines and customers that is worth sharing on the social web.

Armed with our new knowledge of how to research and develop customer personas and the corresponding effects on our content, search, and social media marketing approach, we can next drill down into the finer art of keyword research.

## ACTION ITEMS

1. What are the common characteristics of your best and worst customers?

2. Collect information on your customer segments, including content preferences, search phrases, social networks, and the types of products or services they buy or "like."

3. Based on your research and best-customer characteristics, create and name an "ideal" customer persona for each major group or segment.

4. Map customer needs and goals to your web and social content. Assess performance of existing content and add new content to your editorial plan where needed.

# CHAPTER 7

## Words Are Key to Customers: Keyword Research

"Sandra Manager" is a midlevel marketing manager at a paper supply firm in the Midwest. She is in her early thirties and has 10 years of industry experience, 5 in a supervisory role at her current company. She is active on social networks in her daily life, but struggles with how she can best connect with new customers through social channels.

You work for a start-up software company that offers a customer relationship management (CRM) software product. Its most compelling feature is an ability to integrate with multiple social media platforms. Oh, and "Sandra Manager" has just been given a new software budget.

What's important to realize about "Sandra Manager" is this: She is a persona, or the character you've created to represent your target prospect. Developing your personas by following processes laid out in Chapter 6 will help you see your prospects in a much brighter light. You will be able to theorize on everything from what they had for breakfast that morning to why they can't stand Harry Potter. Essentially, you will know just about everything relevant to your product that could influence your customer personas. But, as an online marketer, unless you combine persona development with keyword research, you will be missing detail regarding one critical factor: the language your prospects use to search and socialize.

Traditional SEO copywriting recommendations often focus on finding and using keywords based primarily on popularity. Clients and consultants often work together to create massive keyword glossaries, or lists consisting of thousands of keywords, each weighted equally in terms of potential impact on driving new business. In many situations, building keyword glossaries skims over categorization, priority, and sometimes even relevance to the customer position in the buying cycle. In these situations, the objective is to capture top search visibility for every keyword on the list. The actual language used by the "Sandra Managers" of the world, or the keywords used to describe "what customers want," can be as different from what business managers and marketers use as the difference between "inexpensive air transportation" and "cheap flights." That disconnect can cost companies millions.

To illustrate how the trend is backing away from one-dimensional keyword evaluation, imagine the following broad-stroke scenario. You are developing a new campaign designed to build awareness of your CRM software's social media integration capabilities. You conduct keyword research and discover that the keyword phrase "Facebook integration" is more popular than keywords related to integration of any other social platform combined. Yet your frontline sales team consistently fields calls asking whether your software "integrates with LinkedIn," which is mirrored by research during persona development. Which phrase should drive your keyword optimization effort? What customers search for and talk about on the social web may be different.

You could make a case for both answers. Because everything in the online world can be tested and revised, the answer you settle on probably won't fall into a bucket neatly labeled as right or wrong. In fact, the only wrong avenue you can take when selecting keywords is to ignore the wealth of data in front of you, including what should be filtered into your initial brainstorm session.

## A PERFECT KEYWORD BRAINSTORM

But before we get too far ahead of ourselves and too far into the minds of our personas, let's discuss factors that can help drive an effective keyword brainstorm session.

A thunderstorm will do the most damage if it can concentrate itself in a targeted location. If it is spread too thin, it dilutes into little more than raindrops. Similarly, the risk of a keyword brainstorm that is allowed to spread unstructured into too many different areas can result in a glossary consisting of thousands of keywords with little thought given to categorization, priority, or customer relevance.

On the other hand, if time is spent on research prior to a keyword brainstorming session, understanding what customer personas care about and which keywords are driving traffic to your own or your competitors' websites, the stage can be set for a powerfully focused brainstorm exercise.

Figure 7.1 illustrates a word cloud of the first steps in a keyword glossary brainstorm. It represents the analysis of a website focused on the paper products industry and five top competitors. Tools used in this analysis included Google Analytics, for analyzing the company's website, and SEMRush, which was used for analyzing the Google keyword ranking of competitor websites. Top nonbranded keywords (i.e., keywords not containing client names) are documented, along with data related to current ranking position, frequency of usage, and percent of total traffic.

After documentation, all keywords are organized into logical clusters by topic and with some consideration for the categories of the company website. Initial research and categorization will ensure your brainstorm begins on a far more productive note than simply posing generalized questions, such as "Which keywords would you like to be found for?"

**FIGURE 7.1   Keyword Brainstorming**

## DOCUMENT KEYWORD METRICS

Throughout this book, I have commented on the need to evolve SEO practices to become more holistic and to take a more customer-centric approach. That said, there are some basic best practices that will remain fundamental, one of which is researching and documenting keyword metrics.

Keyword metrics are analyzed prior to a formal keyword brainstorm when reviewing competitor data and then again when analyzing the resulting list of brainstormed keywords. This task results in three metrics (as shown in Figure 7.2):

1. *Popularity*. A metric culled from second- and third-party panel data using research tools like Keyword Discovery, Wordtracker, or WordStream.

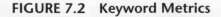

**FIGURE 7.2   Keyword Metrics**

| Keyword Phrase Level 1 | | Popularity (Keyword Discovery) | Global Monthly Search Volume (Google) | Competitiveness (Google) |
|---|---|---|---|---|
| **QA Complete** | | | | |
| **Keyword Glossary** | | | | |
| **Door Hangers** | | | | |
| door hangers | | 95 | 110,000 | 3,390,000 |
| die cut door hangers | | 0 | 140 | 200,000 |
| **Security Paper** | | | | |
| security paper | | 3 | 49,500 | 45,100,000 |
| **Door Hanger Paper** | | | | |
| door hanger paper | | 2 | 1,000 | 1,880,000 |
| door hangers paper | | 0 | 880 | 1,930,000 |
| blank door hanger paper | | 0 | 73 | 304,000 |

**FIGURE 7.3    Keyword Prioritization**

2. *Global monthly search volume.* A metric provided by the Google AdWords Keyword tool as shown in Figure 7.3.
3. *Competitiveness.* The approximate number of unique search results returned on Google and Bing containing an exact match of the keyword phrase in question. Presence of the target keyword in title tags of search results can also be used to refine competitiveness of search results.

These are basic, easy-to-use, and mostly free tools that anyone reading this book can use. As you advance in your pursuit of keyword nirvana, many other, more sophisticated tools are available. Documenting metrics at this stage in the process helps a great deal with prioritization. Initially, keyword categories can be arranged from most popular to least popular, which serves to ensure a more productive initial brainstorm.

## KEYWORD BRAINSTORM, EVALUATION, AND FILTERING

By the time you reach the actual brainstorm stage, it is very likely that you will have many of the final keyword categories already fleshed out.

This will help you ask the easy, yet critical questions that help launch a brainstorming session.

- Are the keywords being used by your competitors important and relevant to your offering?
- Are the keywords currently driving traffic to your website the most relevant?
- What other keywords describe your offering in this category?
- What keywords are good representations of your customer personas' needs and goals?
- What keywords represent the interests of your customer personas according to their position in the buying cycle?

By spending time researching factors ranging from current rankings and frequency of usage by the competition to search volume and competitiveness, you will be armed with the basic data you need to ask the tough questions that can transform an initial brainstorm into deeper keyword usage insight, including:

- Are the initial keyword phrases the language of marketing executives or of your customers?
- Why does your website deserve to have top visibility in this category?
- What is the difference between your initial target keyword list and actual website content?
- Are you prepared to create the amount and quality of content needed to be successful in this category?
- Can you commit to creating and optimizing customer-centric content in this category on an ongoing basis?

## LISTEN TO THE VOICE OF THE CUSTOMER

The last question dovetails nicely into a key step in the keyword brainstorm—a step that is not adequately served by either competitor research or a brainstorm with business executives: the *voice of the customer*.

Let's circle back to our example on the decision to develop a campaign centered on "Facebook integration" or "LinkedIn integration." Without insight provided by frontline employees, the ability of your software to integrate with LinkedIn would likely never have even been up for consideration. After all, traditional metrics would point you toward Facebook.

The voice of the customer, as represented by your research into customer personas, should be weaved into your keyword glossary development process. Involving frontline employees with brainstorming sessions, either directly or through interviews during the persona research process, can open a gold mine of data, ensuring your final keyword glossary is populated with keywords that are not only popular, but also meaningful for your best customers.

## FILTER KEYWORDS WITH A RESEARCH TOOL

Earlier, we touched on third-party keyword research tools that you could use to support the development of your keyword glossary. Before we go further, however, let's start with a few key principles:

- Keyword research tools are designed to support the assumptions provided by the two most powerful keyword tools that you access: *research* (with customers, prospects, and frontline employees) and *relevance* (to the brand product and services mix).
- Keyword research tools are designed to override the false assumptions often provided by the two most flawed tools that you can access—your gut and your brain.
- Keyword research tools listed in this chapter represent only a handful of examples pulled from a variety of tools available.

If you are developing a keyword glossary using this chapter as a guide, it is very likely that you are now staring at a large list of keywords, categorized according to time spent on competitive, brand, and customer research.

If you are feeling overwhelmed at this point, that's okay. In fact, it's very nearly ideal. This means that you have a very large list of powerful and impactful keywords in front of you. All you have to do now is refine them into a workable format. This is where you need to suspend your two most dangerous tools—head and gut—in favor of third-party tools that will help you see these phrases efficiently and objectively.

Let's look at an example of how a keyword category, "social media + CRM integration," might appear after an initial brainstorm session, as shown in Figure 7.4.

| CRM Software |
|---|
| crm software |
| Social crm software |
| crm software social media integration |
| integrating social media with crm software |
| facebook crm software integration |
| linkedin crm software integration |
| twitter crm software integration |
| facebook crm |
| linkedin crm |
| twitter crm |
| facebook crm integration |
| twitter crm integration |
| linkedin crm integration |

**FIGURE 7.4  Keyword Categories for Social Media + CRM Integration Key Phrases**

In this category, both "CRM software" and "software CRM" would serve as examples of *broad* phrases, whereas "social CRM software" would represent a *long-tail* phrase. A broad phrase would refer to the most popular and usually shortest keyword variation within a category. The long-tail phrase, on the other hand, is a more specific, multiword phrase related to the broad phrase.

It should be noted here that on an individual basis, long-tail phrases will commonly generate less individual search volume than broader phrases. For example, the Google AdWords Keyword Tool reports that "CRM software" has 74,000 local monthly searches and that "small business CRM software" has 2,400. If the focus of your CRM software company is on small businesses, then it makes a lot more sense to be relevant if you're interested in attracting new business more quickly. Considering the pain points, needs, and goals of your customer according to their position in the buying cycle is also an important consideration when filtering for more specific search phrases.

There's a tendency for searchers to use specific three- or four-word long-tail phrases in their search engine queries. In fact, over 50 percent of search phrases are three words or longer.[1] Why do long-tail phrases get so little search volume? Because very few people use the same long-tail phrases.

For example, while we optimize our site at TopRankBlog.com for a mix of 15 to 20 phrases, we actually receive organic search traffic from more than 28,000 unique phrases each month. Many of those phrases were used only once or twice during the entire month. Another perspective is the fact that 16 percent of the daily queries on Google have never been seen before.[2] That means there are a lot of long-tail phrases out there.

Later in this book, we will offer more tips on how to determine which long-tail keywords to add to your glossary, how to track them, and how to use them in content development efforts.

The keyword category discussed here represents just one of dozens on your list, with each category consisting of a similar number of keywords. At this stage in the development of your keyword glossary, you'll want to remember this phrase: "Those who strive to be everything to everyone will be nothing to anyone." In other words, *focus*. Find ways to filter keyword variations in your initial brainstormed list that offer no immediate benefit, while fleshing out your categories with phrases that carry more impact.

While you can start to whittle down your list with the help of several tools, the one I share here is Keyword Discovery. This keyword research and project management tool pulls search popularity metrics gathered from second- and third-party panel data. Basically a sample of search queries used to estimate popularity, Keyword Discovery is also useful for providing alternative variations of keywords that you may not have considered. (See Figure 7.5.)

Based solely on data provided here, "CRM software" would appear to be the most attractive broad phrase, whereas searches for social-focused

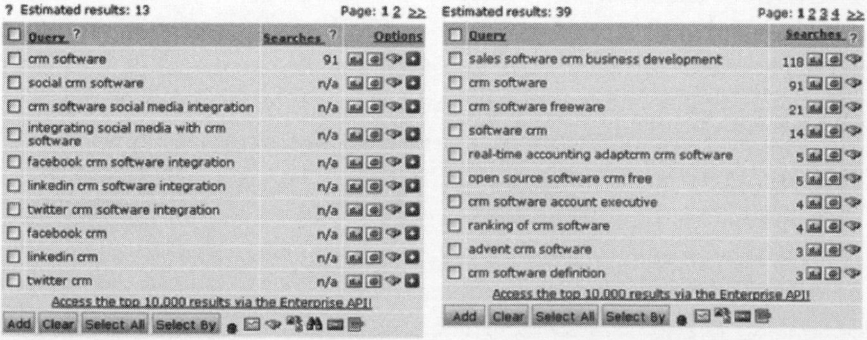

**FIGURE 7.5    Keyword Discovery**

keywords have not been substantial enough over the past 12 months to register any kind of popularity score within this tool. In regard to derivative phrases research, we can determine at a glance that there is some searcher tendency to use both "CRM software" and the variation "software CRM" when searching.

Another insight we can glean from this data is that searcher interest appears to be lacking for keywords related to "social" + "CRM." Of course, you know this can't be the whole picture. After all, your frontline sales team fields calls daily related to integration of your CRM software with very specific social platforms, and the social integration module is one of your highest-selling features. It's time to turn to another tool to put these numbers into context.

The Google AdWords Keyword Tool provides detail regarding the estimated volume of monthly searches happening on Google for a keyword, both globally and locally, on average over the past 12 months. Because this data is provided primarily for the benefit of advertisers, there is a vested interest in updating this data frequently. So, what context does Google AdWords give us on our list of keywords in Figure 7.6?

Much like the information we gathered from Keyword Discovery, Google AdWords Keyword Tool is telling us that "CRM software" is

| Search terms (14) | | | |
|---|---|---|---|
| Keyword | Competition | Global Monthly Searches | Local Monthly Searches |
| ☆ crm software | High | 201,000 | 74,000 |
| ☆ software crm | High | 201,000 | 74,000 |
| ☆ social crm software | High | 480 | 140 |
| ☆ crm software social media integration | - | - | - |
| ☆ integrating social media with crm software | - | - | - |
| ☆ facebook crm software integration | - | - | - |
| ☆ linkedin crm software integration | - | - | - |
| ☆ twitter crm software integration | - | - | - |
| ☆ facebook crm | Medium | 3,600 | 390 |
| ☆ linkedin crm | Low | 2,900 | 1,000 |
| ☆ twitter crm | Low | 1,000 | 260 |
| ☆ facebook crm integration | Low | 170 | 36 |
| ☆ twitter crm integration | Low | 73 | 16 |
| ☆ linkedin crm integration | Low | 110 | 46 |

**FIGURE 7.6   Google AdWords Estimated Volume**

our most popular phrase and that volume around social-related keywords trails far behind.

That said, volume around broad, social-related keywords is certainly not nil, and many keywords related to specific platforms are generating between 1,000 and 3,600 global monthly searches. While our extremely targeted long-tail keywords (e.g., "Facebook CRM integration") capture fewer than 100 global searches per month in some cases, these phrases could be used editorially in content that supports the more popular keyword variations (e.g., "Facebook CRM"). Also, keep in mind how relevant a phrase is and that our research is just a snapshot in time. The popularity of a particular phrase could rise, fall or fluctuate according to seasonality and demand due to news stories and trends in popular culture. If phrases appear with nominal query volume but have appeared in your persona research with customers and frontline employees, and if the conversion rates for those niche phrases are very high, it makes sense to include them in your glossary.

Based on the research conducted to date, our keyword category on "Social CRM" might be whittled down to the list shown in Figure 7.7.

| | Popularity/ Searches (From Keyword Discovery) | Global Monthly Search Volume (From Google AdWords) |
|---|---|---|
| **CRM Software** | | |
| crm software | 91 | 201,000 |
| software crm | 14 | 201,000 |
| facebook crm | 0 | 3,600 |
| linkedin crm | 0 | 2,900 |
| twitter crm | 0 | 1,000 |
| social crm software | 0 | 480 |
| facebook crm integration | 0 | 170 |
| linkedin crm integration | 0 | 110 |
| twitter crm integration | 0 | 73 |

**FIGURE 7.7   Keyword Category for Social CRM**

Although we have managed to refine this category down to a more targeted list, there are two basic questions to answer in terms of assessing the viability of our keyword glossary:

1. What is the likelihood that I will capture a first-page position for a keyword phrase?
2. If I do capture a top spot, what is the likelihood that this phrase will lead to a visit, a microconversion, an inquiry, or a sale?

To answer these questions, we turn to another tool that, like our brain and our gut, is powerful and accessible by all: the search engine. Spending a few minutes searching Google or Bing for a keyword can instantly give you a hint at how much general competition you are up against and what the competitive landscape of the search results looks like. As we discussed in Chapter 3 on research, there is a difference between business competition and content competition in search results. Evaluate the sources as well as the types of content that appear in the search results for the keyword phrase in question to assist in your decision about the viability.

Look at searches for "CRM software" with more than 43 million search results on Google and "software CRM" with more than 185 million search results. Both phrases indicated a significant amount of search volume according to both Keyword Discovery and Google AdWords. That means there is likely a significant amount of traffic potential for each phrase if you can achieve top search visibility and awareness. But how difficult will it be to meet that goal?

Despite the keywords being rather similar in terms of meaning and likely in terms of searcher intent, there is a large chasm in terms of competition. Does it make sense to try to go after a broad keyword already in competition with 185 million other pages, or to try to concentrate on a similarly broad phrase that's working against the smaller, yet formidable, group of 43 million pages? Assuming equal or greater relevance and demand, the option offering less competition is an attractive choice.

Next, let's look at search results and competition associated with more specific keywords. (See Figure 7.8.)

Results for "Facebook CRM" show heavy competition—but also top competitors such as Salesforce.com. "Twitter CRM," meanwhile, shows a high level of competition combined with editorial and resource-based

|  | Popularity/ Searches (From Keyword Discovery) | Global Monthly Search Volume (From Google AdWords) | Competitiveness (From Google) |
|---|---|---|---|
| **CRM Software** |  |  |  |
| crm software | 91 | 201,000 | 8,680,000 |
| facebook crm | 0 | 3,600 | 93,800,000 |
| linkedin crm | 0 | 2,900 | 37,200,000 |
| twitter crm | 0 | 1,000 | 89,300,000 |
| social crm software | 0 | 480 | 29,900,000 |
| facebook crm integration | 0 | 170 | 8,810,000 |
| linkedin crm integration | 0 | 110 | 5,730,000 |
| twitter crm integration | 0 | 73 | 9,000,000 |

**FIGURE 7.8   Keyword Competitiveness**

results from TechCrunch and Mashable. Finally, "LinkedIn CRM" search results show the most reasonable level of competition when compared against Facebook- and Twitter-related keyword phrases. "LinkedIn CRM," like "Twitter CRM," search results are mostly populated with resource-based content.

It should be noted that basing keyword decisions or SEO success purely on keyword ranking is inherently flawed. At any given time, Google has hundreds of algorithms in the wild that impact ranking results, creating the possibility of a different result nearly anytime a search is conducted, not to mention the impact of geographic location, personalization, and Google+ search plus Your World. So, what we are striving to determine is not just who is ranking, but rather a flavor for how much and what type of content is ranking relevant to the interests and goals of our target audience. What we can infer from our research:

- Those searching for "Facebook CRM" are more likely looking to buy.
- Those searching for "LinkedIn CRM" and "Twitter CRM" are more likely looking to learn.
- The popularity and searcher intent behind these keywords is not a secret to competing websites.

Based on all of the research here, we can make a case for nearly every keyword in the category we are working with. Since we cannot reasonably make a case for removing any keywords from this category, how do we ensure we don't fall into the trap of trying to be everything to everyone? Let's start by changing the conversation.

## BUILDING YOUR KEYWORD GLOSSARY

Everything we've spoken about so far in this chapter has focused on one outcome: development of a prioritized, categorized, and manageable keyword glossary that is as considerate of customer interests as those of the company selling products and services. This glossary will be the cornerstone of your search engine optimization efforts that guide SEO copywriting applied to existing content, the suggestion of new content, and optimization of social media content. But first, let's get back to our original question of refining the keyword category.

The category we are working with has been fleshed out in Figure 7.9 to include a metric defining competitiveness using the simplistic method of approximate number of pages that appear in the search results when the target phrase is searched on Google.

Those on your team who have not subjected themselves to the research you just conducted may see the list as one make-sense category. All keywords speak to social integration and can be used to describe the social integration capabilities of your software. But in spending time out in the wild, you know that the search landscape and searcher intent behind these keywords is a much different story. For instance:

- Competition for "CRM Software"-related keywords are reasonably competitive.
- Competition for "Facebook CRM" and "Twitter CRM" are extraordinarily high, while far more reasonable for "LinkedIn CRM."
- Atop a large number of search results for "Facebook CRM" and "Twitter CRM" are your top business competitors.
- Atop a large number of search results for "Twitter CRM" and a reasonable number of search results for "LinkedIn CRM" are resource- and article-based results.
- "LinkedIn CRM integration" represents a potential third-party hole in the search landscape.

| | Popularity/ Searches (From Keyword Discovery) | Global Monthly Search Volume (From Google AdWords) | Competitiveness (From Google) |
|---|---|---|---|
| **CRM Software** | | | |
| crm software | 91 | 201,000 | 8,680,000 |
| social crm software | 0 | 480 | 29,900,000 |

| | Popularity/ Searches (From Keyword Discovery) | Global Monthly Search Volume (From Google AdWords) | Competitiveness (From Google) |
|---|---|---|---|
| facebook crm | 0 | 3,600 | 93,800,000 |
| facebook crm integration | 0 | 170 | 8,810,000 |

| | Popularity/ Searches (From Keyword Discovery) | Global Monthly Search Volume (From Google AdWords) | Competitiveness (From Google) |
|---|---|---|---|
| linkedin crm | 0 | 2,900 | 37,200,000 |
| linkedin crm integration | 0 | 110 | 5,730,000 |

| | Popularity/ Searches (From Keyword Discovery) | Global Monthly Search Volume (From Google AdWords) | Competitiveness (From Google) |
|---|---|---|---|
| twitter crm | 0 | 1,000 | 89,300,000 |
| twitter crm integration | 0 | 73 | 9,000,000 |

**FIGURE 7.9   Competitive Keyword Categories**

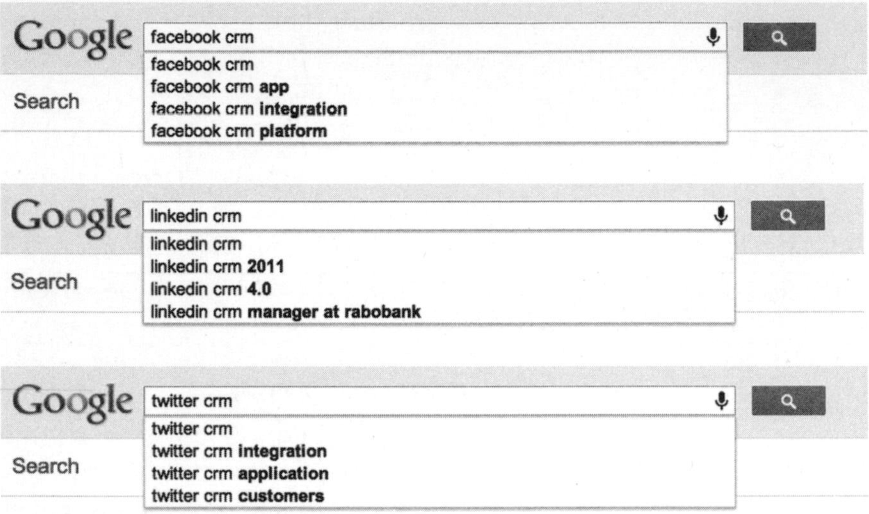

**FIGURE 7.10  Google Suggest**

In other words, you are not looking at one unmanageable keyword category. Instead, you are looking at several categories.

When building your keyword glossary, breaking up larger categories into more focused and manageable categories is one of the surest ways to effectively determine which keywords should be used in content optimization efforts, which keywords should be used to drive what type of content (think of a web page designed to sell a product versus a blog post designed to educate about a subject), and the priority in which these keywords should fall.

As we get more into a conversation regarding priority, or when we start to discuss which keywords will drive a significant portion of your optimization and promotional efforts, it's time to once again put some trust in your brain and your gut. But this doesn't mean that there aren't some tools at your disposal that can help your efforts.

Two tools you can use most readily are tools that are freely available and courtesy of Google. The first is one you may not have considered.

Google Suggest is represented by autocompleting queries that occur when you type letters into Google's search box based on a mix of data sources. (See Figure 7.10.) Google Suggest can provide you with insight into which keyword variations are trending upward, even though you lack search volume metrics reported by other third-party research tools.

Based on the screenshots shown in Figure 7.10, taken from Google Suggest using our three social platform CRM-specific phrases, there is some support that backs up our decision to use each phrase. In regard to prioritization—and this is a bit off the cuff—it appears that those searching for "Twitter CRM" and "LinkedIn CRM" are more likely to add "integration" as a modifier than those searching for "Facebook CRM." The simple reason behind this assumption is that "Facebook CRM app" currently appears higher than "Facebook CRM integration" in Google Suggest data.

Of course, the flip side of this real-time coin is that these results may be somewhat different the next time you look. Which is why, again, no one tool should be trusted to guide all of your decisions. Since Google Suggest displays suggestions in a format that you cannot copy, there is a very useful tool, called ubersuggest.org, based on Google Suggest data that allows you to export a deep list of suggested phrases organized in alphabetical order as a text file. This will make it much easier to bring Google Suggest keywords into your glossary document, which will likely be Excel.

Another tool you can leverage, and one that provides more data in regard to forecasting, is Google Insights for Search. (See Figure 7.11.) Offering a past and future trend line related to a keyword, Google Insight for Search can help you make prioritization-based decisions taking into account both what has happened and what is likely to happen.

One limitation with this tool, however, is that keywords with a lower search volume (e.g., "Facebook CRM integration") won't register data. As such, the examples are pulled using the broader "CRM"-based terms rather than the more specific "CRM integration"-based phrases.

As shown in Figure 7.11, again, you can make a case to put these keyword categories in any priority order. But remember the beginning of our story. Which of these variations do your customers currently ask about? (Answer: "LinkedIn.")

What we know from our keyword research so far is:

- There is a fair amount of search volume surrounding "CRM integration" of all social platforms.
- Traffic related to each social platform phrase variation is forecast to improve.

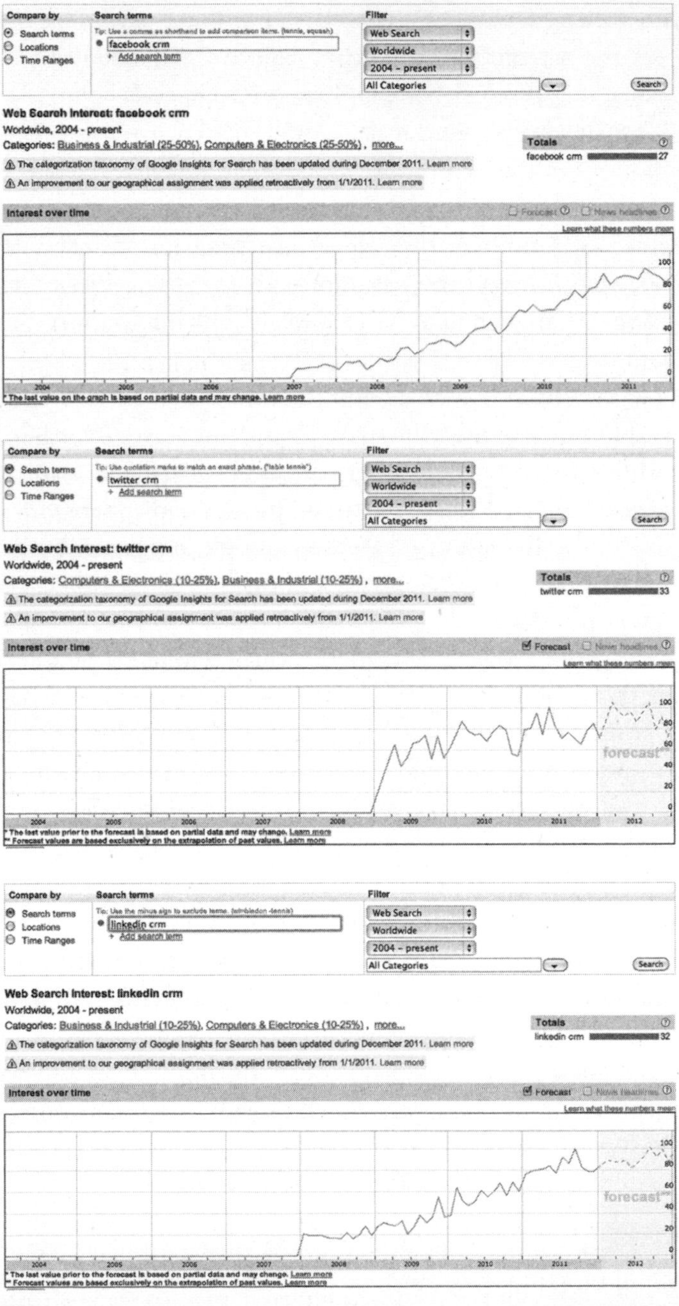

FIGURE 7.11    Google Insights for Search

- Facebook is by far the most popular and the most competitive modifier, with Twitter following closely behind.
- There may be a hole atop the market for LinkedIn phrases.
- Customers are asking about LinkedIn-related content.

By conducting the necessary research and using the valuable customer insight provided by your frontline team, you can make a reasonable case to focus your optimization and content development efforts on "LinkedIn CRM" integration-related phrases as one of your primary keyword phrase segments. At the same time, you can focus appropriate efforts on your software's ability to integrate with other social platforms as well.

Now complete this exercise with the rest of your keyword list to refine and prioritize the balance of brainstormed phrases. Then spend time with stakeholders to help finalize the list. Keep in mind that with very large websites, this has to be done initially at the top category levels of content. Additionally, you may have keyword clusters defined by your business objectives and key goals for customer personas that will guide prioritization of a large body of keywords.

Regardless of the size of website or number of target keyword phrases, it's important to understand that this is not meant to be an overnight process. What you are building is a keyword list that will remain in place as a starting point of reference for your content optimization, social media optimization, and link building for the next 6 to 12 months. Depending on your resources and ability to implement optimization on existing content as well as with new content, it can take some time before implementation effects are observed through improved search positioning, traffic, and links. Data collected from content marketing performance in search will enable further keyword list refinement as well as content creation, optimization, and promotion. When properly developed, a keyword glossary is an exceptional tool that can provide specific and actionable information applicable to any content creation activity in the organization, from marketing to customer service.

## RESEARCH SOCIAL TOPICS

After this exercise, what you should have in front of you is a beautifully crafted, prioritized keyword glossary designed to guide your content optimization, creation, and promotion efforts for the next several months.

That covers search, but what about social? Depending on the need or situation, consumers may follow a pure search path to conversion. However, consumers are increasingly influenced by content they find on social media and networks as well as requested recommendations from friends. The consumer journey from initial query to purchase is increasingly complex, involving a combination of social interaction and research on search engines. The good news is that your initial category and competitive research, in combination with the work developing customer personas, will reveal insights about which social channels and topics matter most to your customers.

In combination with search keyword research, the next step in our process to become the most relevant source of information about our category of business is to develop a dynamic list of social topics. In other words, search engine optimization will guide us to the party, but social topics will help us be more interesting once we get there. If we can gauge demand for search phrases with keyword research tools, why not tap into what the most popular topics are on the social web, relevant to your business and solutions?

For an understanding of how a social keyword list can be developed, let's use the high-priority keyword phrase we identified previously, "LinkedIn CRM integration," and conduct a very basic search using real-time social engine SocialMention.com. While there are other social media monitoring or listening tools that can extract social keyword topics from their reports, they often carry substantial monthly fees. I've picked Social Mention for our example here because it's free and easy to use. It can be a great starting point for getting your feet wet with social topic research. Other free tools that can provide insight into popular social topics include:

- http://www.stumbleupon.com/tag/. A more popular bookmarking service, this page shows the most recently popular tags and the most popular of all time.
- http://technorati.com/tag/. For blog topics, this is an organized directory of the most popular tags used on Technorati over the past month.
- https://ads.youtube.com/keyword_tool. YouTube is social media at it's finest, and this tool is specifically for finding the most popular search phrases used to find videos.

- www.hashtags.org. Hashtags (#) are often used on Twitter as a sort of folksonomy of categorization. This tool shows a weekly trend of any hashtag you search on.

Social Mention will gather results from sources ranging from Twitter to blogs and comments, aggregating information as recent a few hours old. (See Figure 7.12.) Social Mention will also provide an indication of how searchers are consuming information by showing the most popular social channels relevant to your search.

So, what can we learn about "LinkedIn CRM integration" from Social Mention?

A glance at the search results shows a diversity of content sources, including Twitter, YouTube, Facebook, and Delicious. Within that content, we

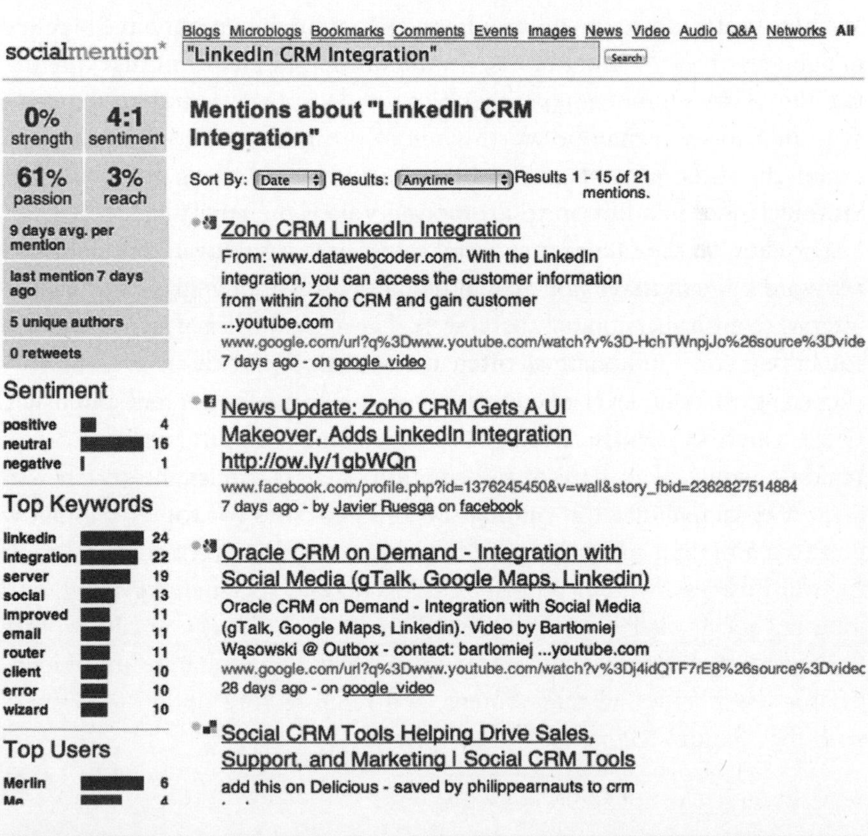

**FIGURE 7.12   Social Mention**

can see customer survey capabilities are sparking discussion. Also, building deep customer insights is a benefit of note. We can see that LinkedIn, Dell, and Salesforce will be among the competitors to keep an eye on.

Based on this basic exercise for one target keyword phrase using Social Mention, we can develop a list of social topics including:

- LinkedIn CRM integration customer survey capabilities
- LinkedIn CRM integration helps build consumer insights
- LinkedIn CRM integration competitor comparisons
- LinkedIn CRM integration trends
- LinkedIn CRM integration blended with Facebook and Twitter integration
- LinkedIn CRM integration demo

These social topics can guide whatever content you might have planned in support of the "LinkedIn CRM integration" keyword phrase, including blog posts, comments on other blogs, videos, tweets, and bookmarks. We can also see it may be worthwhile to promote that content through social channels, such as social bookmarking, and news sites, such as StumbleUpon, in addition to promoting videos on YouTube.

The icing on the cake is that social topics are useful for adding long-tail keyword content that's not only in demand on search engines but also of interest to customers on the social web. The dynamic list of social topics is something you can update as often as necessary—weekly or even daily—according to your level of activity as a social media content publisher. Once search keywords are in place with content optimization and link building, you have a base of information to attract relevant search visitors. A proactive effort at mining social media sites for topics will allow you to maintain a more dynamic list of ideas and conversations relevant to your business, which can inspire new content, social engagement, and long-tail social media optimization. Once implemented, you can capture data for refinement, which Chapter 13 will help you with in terms of identifying new phrases, testing content, and refining your ability to connect with the "Sandra Managers" of the world.

## ACTION ITEMS

1. Based on your research into customer segments and personas, identify top level keyword ideas for phrases that represent topics relevant to your major products and services.

2. Brainstorm a mix of keywords and phrases based on site content, product, and services mix and by surveying front line employees. Organize that brainstormed list into an Excel spreadsheet.

3. Identify keyword popularity by importing your list of phrases into a keyword research tool like Google AdWords Keyword Tool, Wordtracker, Wordstream, or Keyword Discovery.

4. Assess keywords as broad or long tail and map then to relevant content on your website. Filter phrases to focus on relevance, competitiveness, and popularity.

5. Use a social search tool like socialmention.com to identify possible social topics to augment search keyword lists.

# CHAPTER 8

CHAPTER 8

## Attract, Engage, and Inspire: Building Your Content Plan

What a journey we're on. We've identified our goals and know who our customers are as well as what they care about in terms of search keywords and social topics. Now it's time to translate that planning, research, and insight into an actionable content plan.

### WHAT IS CONTENT MARKETING?

Content marketing is an approach to attract, engage, and inspire customers to a logical conclusion to buy and share through content that empathizes with the varied interests and behaviors during the buying cycle.

As a marketing discipline, content marketing has skyrocketed in popularity, with over 60 percent of content marketers planning to increase their spend over the next 12 months.[1] It's no wonder content has stepped into the spotlight, as consumers have become numb to the overabundance of traditional advertising and now spend more time educating themselves online about products and services before they buy. Content is the reason search engines exist, and it's also a common vehicle for social sharing in the form of text, images, video, and audio. When marketers can effectively align their knowledge of search and social keyword demand with a relevant content plan, it helps connect buyers with products and services more efficiently, thus resulting in a better customer experience. There's no doubt that content is the key to more effective online marketing. The question is, "How do we to plan, create, optimize, promote, and measure a content marketing plan that helps our brand become the most relevant choice for our target audience?"

## KNOWING YOUR CUSTOMER IS ESSENTIAL FOR EFFECTIVE CONTENT MARKETING

Chief Manufacturing is a leading provider of professional AV solutions to dealers and distributors across several industries, including education, health care, and hospitality. In order to improve the effectiveness of their content marketing, Chief needed to identify key differences in the customer preferences for information and communication. The target audiences for Chief include dealers and installers, each with unique characteristics worth considering when developing content plans.

Focus groups revealed that dealers were starting to skew slightly younger than in the past. With the changing demographics, dealers were increasingly savvy about online sources of information, including reading blogs and other forms of digital communications. This trend did not hold true for dealers who skewed slightly older and still preferred to receive print communications.

The second target audience, installers, was similarly split as far as age range and type of content consumption, resulting in the tendency to look for a different type of information. Whereas dealers were more open to receiving sales-oriented content and product overviews, the installers were more interested in receiving how-to information about the product, including specifications and installation details. The marketing group at Chief understood that the installers have the ear of the dealers, so providing easy-to-use documentation for Chief's solutions was a priority to ensure that the dealers continued to select Chief products.

As Chief developed its content marketing strategy, it was essential to identify the needs of each target audience, types of content they prefer to consume, and the feedback loop between the two audiences and how that might impact future purchases.

The result was a content plan that outlined unique concepts and delivery mechanisms for each audience that positioned Chief for success in communicating core messages about its offerings as the most relevant choice for each distinct customer segment.

The Chief Manufacturing story is a simple example that illustrates the importance of understanding different customer groups and then planning content accordingly to increase marketing effectiveness at inspiring sales as well as developing better customer relationships.

## IS YOUR MARKETING MECHANICAL OR MEANINGFUL?

Most companies are more than happy to increase leads and sales with good content marketing. But what about fostering better customer relationships? What about better customer satisfaction, lowered costs for support, and an increase in both retention and referrals? Whatever the reason companies publish content online, that content can leverage keyword optimization for better visibility where prospects, employees, or customers are looking. Social discovery and sharing of content is another opportunity for companies to better connect their messages and value with communities that are interested. Business value from optimized and socialized content marketing comes in many forms, and to get a good picture of what that means, it's important to understand the role of content across the customer life cycle. (See Figure 8.1.)

*Awareness*. Content marketing contributes to the development of brand awareness by helping people find your product or service through search, social media, or wherever content can play a role as an information source.

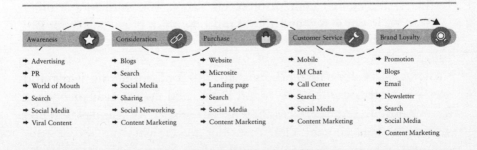

**FIGURE 8.1  Customer and Content Life Cycle**

*Consideration.* Once prospects know about your brand and solutions, content can educate them on your unique selling proposition. Content provided on your website, blog, social media networks, and other online platforms should make it easy for prospects and customers to understand your advantages and key benefits. A strong search and social media presence can boost credibility and shorten sales cycles.

*Purchase.* The prominent visibility of your content for long-tail search queries that represent a specific intent to purchase is essential with any website that is expected to attract new business. Once you've gained customers' trust and respect and they have decided to purchase from you, it's not the end of the line for content marketing and optimization. There's more work you can do in terms of refining the effectiveness of your content's ability to produce inquires and sales. Website statistics analysis and online sales paths that track the content viewed by your customer before purchase can assist with refining everything from the keyword focus of your search and social media optimization to optimizing for improved conversion performance.

*Service.* Content and social applications encourage customers to have a great experience on your site, even when they aren't making a purchase. As we discussed in previous chapters, content like FAQs and other information about your brand offers customers a baseline postpurchase support service they can turn to at any time of day to find answers without having to contact one of your customer service resources. Making it easy for customers to find answers to their questions can save on your support costs and lead to better customer satisfaction.

*Loyalty.* People love your products; they visit your website; they engage with you on social networks. Each of their interactions with your content offers even more insights into the motivations and interests of your customers. Newsletters, webinars, helpful how-to articles, and similar content offerings that help customers get more out of their purchases and the brand relationship can foster loyalty above and beyond the competition.

The value of content marketing goes beyond attracting leads and sales—to fostering goodwill, brand value, and empowerment of fans to refer products and services they like to others. As you develop and implement your content plan, consider the holistic impact of content on reaching and engaging with your customers throughout the relationship.

## CREATE A CONTENT PLAN

With an understanding of our business and marketing goals, target consumer personas, and how those insights translate into keywords and topics, we are ready to create an optimized and socialized content plan.

Consumers tend to engage with information that is most interesting, timely, and relevant to them. Content marketing isn't as simple as publishing and distributing what you think potential customers want to see. There has to be some sort of order and strategy in place to achieve mutually beneficial results. An editorial calendar is vital to any content marketing effort for bringing together your understanding of customer goals and the key benefits of your products into a schedule of useful content and media creation.

Traditional media outlets such as television news, newspapers, and magazines use editorial calendars to plan the types of stories they will cover. The goal of these calendars is to secure a steady stream of fresh content consistently into the future. They also ensure the content is relevant and suits the needs of content producers, readers, and advertisers.

Editorial calendars for content marketing purposes are very similar. To create one, it takes an understanding of the communities and individuals you're trying to reach. Our discussion of personas in Chapter 6 covered most of that homework, but it's essentially about researching customer preferences in terms of content discovery, consumption, and engagement. It's also about answering some important questions: What are your target customer's needs and goals? What do they search for, and what do they talk about on the social web relevant to your solution? The insights from those answers are condensed into topics and keyword ideas. Relevant search keywords that are descriptive of the brand, products, or services along with the relevant topics of interest to customers on the social web are analyzed for popularity and competitiveness. This insight is then synthesized and organized into an editorial calendar.

## INVENTORY EXISTING CONTENT AND MAP THE GAPS

Our objective is to not only create new content, but also to leverage all of our online content to build business value for prospects and customers. Taking an inventory of current content assets, including website, social presence, microsites, and other media, helps us understand where gaps

| Date | Title | Topic/Category | Keywords, Tags | Media | Media | Repost | Repost |
|------|-------|----------------|----------------|-------|-------|--------|--------|
| 2/6/12 Mon | Managing Content Marketing for B2B | Content Marketing | B2B, Marketing, Content | Image | | Newsletter | |
| 2/7/12 Tues | Twitter chats | Social Media, Twitter | Twitter Chat, Twitter Marketing | Image | | | |
| 2/8/12 Wed | MarketingSherpa SEO Guide Review | SEO | SEO Guide, Report | Image | video | | |
| 2/9/12 Thur | BIGLIST SEO Blog Reviews 091810 | SEO Blog Review | SEO Blogs | Image | | | |
| 2/10/12 Fri | 5 Tips on social media advertising | Social Media, Advertising | Social Media Avertising | Image | | Newsletter | |
| 2/13/12 Mon | Facebook Marketing Basics & Tools | Social Media | Facebook Marketing, Tools | Image | PPT | | |
| 2/14/12 Tues | Spotlight on Search: (Influential Person) from Famous B | Search Marketing Interview | Enterprise SEO | Image | | | Compile quotes |
| 2/15/12 Wed | Book Review: Title by (Influential Person) | Social Media, Book Review | Social Media Marketing | Image | video | | Compile quotes |
| 2/16/12 Thur | B2B Thursday: Social Media | B2B, Social Media | B2B Social Media, B2B Marketing | Image | | Newsletter | |
| 2/17/12 Fri | 5 Tips on social ecommerce | Social Commerce | Social Media, Social Commerce | Image | | | |

TopRank Online Marketing — Sample Editorial Schedule for a Marketing Blog. See http://www.toprankblog.com for many more tips on SEO, Social & Content Marketing

**FIGURE 8.2   Blog Editorial Plan**

exist between those topics we've already covered and are known for in search, social, and within the target community and those we have not covered, or perhaps covered inadequately. This research will help identify content topics of priority where there is a high degree of interest and relevance for our customers and insufficient content in place to meet that demand. The editorial and content plan addresses those gaps to ensure we are publishing relevant, useful, and shareable content that supports overall brand messaging and business goals, as well as inspiring readers to take the actions we desire. (See Figure 8.2.)

## BASIC PROCESS FOR CREATING AN EDITORIAL CALENDAR

**Determine topics of interest.** Topical relevance is essential for meeting customers' needs, answering questions, and motivating return visits, whether topics are directly about your brand or related information that customers can benefit from. Research into customer segments, persona development, and keyword research will reveal a gold mine of such topics. Typically, we work with primary topics and supporting, or secondary, topics.

For example, Widgets might be a primary topic, but color variations, sizes, applications, end benefits, specifications, and other value attributes, as defined by customer research, would represent secondary topics.

**Create content categories.** Your topics of interest will be divided into certain categories chosen by you to provide some continuity and organization to your published content. Typical categories for an editorial calendar can include breaking headlines, industry news, ongoing series, feature stories, in-depth product or service reports, polls, special promotions, events, tips, lists, and more depending on platforms available for publishing and editorial direction for customer segments.

**Assign content types.** Editorial plans are typically developed for a primary publishing platform like a website, special resources section, blog, or microsite. Some content will live on the company website or blog and other content will publish elsewhere, such as on social media platforms like YouTube, Facebook or Pinterest. Content types within the publishing platform that represent topics of interest can vary according to customer preferences. Articles, videos, images, long-form content, short-form content, and many more formats are possible. I've listed 30 different content types later in this chapter to give you some ideas. The important thing is to be *relevant*: to your customers, your brand, and to search engines and social communities with the content types, formats, and topics you choose.

**Establish a timeline.** It makes sense to prepare a regular publishing schedule according to your resources and the expectations of your targeted customers. At the same time, business often fluctuates or possesses varied timelines due to seasonality, sales cycles, and changes in the industry or company. Allow in your timeline for wildcard content and for adaptations to your schedule. Things may simply come up that you'll want to define within days or weeks (versus three or six months in advance). Regarding seasonality, ask yourself: Is there a product or service you offer that is particularly popular at a certain time of the year? Is a holiday approaching that might influence your target customer? Consider the overarching theme of your content structure as it pertains to the calendar and cyclicality of your business as well as a consistent and regular publishing schedule.

**Chart a publishing schedule.** Take all of the information from the previous steps and organize it into a plan for creating your content. Whatever your publishing method, whether you want to create videos, blogs, articles, or other media, design a schedule that allows you to keep up a certain regularity and that allows you to cross-promote your content between media and publishing channels. For example, a blog post, press release, and video on a very similar topic could all cross-link or make reference to an authoritative report or e-book. If you have dedicated copywriting resources, assign topics or beats for them to cover so they can build up some consistency and expertise in those areas of focus.

**Incorporate other marketing plans.** As with any marketing effort, content marketing practices should integrate with other marketing, advertising, and PR efforts. That could include online and offline communication tools and media. It's not just about marketing, either. The content published by customer service, human resources, public relations, and other departments may offer opportunities to cross-promote as well. Depending on the size and structure of your company, it may make sense to create an informal content council to meet at least quarterly to talk about how you can work together across different departments in the organization to leverage resources and cross-promote.

**Continue the process.** After you've designed your content marketing plan and have started creating, optimizing, and promoting great content, it is time to head back to the beginning. Evaluate your content effectiveness to determine the topics that most interest customers and inspire intended outcomes like shares, referrals, engagement, network growth, leads, and sales. Expand on categories that are popular, pull back on those that fail to perform, and fill in the gaps where your content might be incomplete. Create a cycle of creation, publishing, interaction, analysis, and refinement.

A well-planned, thoughtful, and adaptable content plan can be instrumental for online marketing performance, making an editorial calendar essential. You might not consider your company to be a publisher, but that's exactly what it becomes when you embark on an organized content marketing effort.

## SOCIAL CONTENT PROMOTION

With a content plan in hand, it is time to take a closer look at social content promotion. Search engine optimization passively attracts relevant traffic to your content. Social media promotion and networking actively solicits and invites them to it. The added benefit of social media promotion integrated with search engine optimization is that social sites can send traffic to your content, and they can also provide signals to search engines that will positively affect your natural search engine positioning. Social Media and SEO are working together more closely than ever for companies that are marketing through content online.

A social content promotion plan outlines and provides guidance towards how content will be shared on online networks that have the most potential to attract traffic for your content.

Understanding which social networks your customers are spending time on is important for social promotion, but there's another target audience they may be even more important. The irony is that this group is most often overlooked by companies evaluating whether they should participate in the social web. What group am I talking about? *Influencers.*

Well-connected bloggers or participants on specific social channels relevant to your topics of focus can deliver significant and qualified traffic to the content you're promoting. Some companies might say, "Our customers are not on Twitter or Facebook. They don't read blogs." What's important is whether those individuals who influence your customers are themselves influenced by content they consume on the social web. Of course it's ideal when both customers and influencers can be found in rich dialog on a certain social channel, but customers are not always active participants. Influence is a very valuable currency on the social web, and creating relationships with individuals involved in relevant networks who can in turn influence those in your category can be very productive for content promotion. We cover more about social network development in Chapter 11, but know that content promotion through social channels is an essential part of your content marketing plan.

Social media in general can be a powerful force for influencing today's technology-savvy consumers. As with any marketing plan, creating a strategy for social media promotion can make a huge difference in the distribution and reach of your content.

## 20 DIFFERENT CONTENT TYPES

Content doesn't have to be limited to text and images. Different types of content can appeal to diverse types of people and serve varying purposes. Any content that can be optimized for better visibility on search engines can also be shareable with social. As I like to say, "Optimize for search, optimize for share."

One of the biggest challenges for companies is the creation of content. Yet content creation is one of the most effective SEO tactics.[2] To help generate ideas for the types of content you might consider with your content marketing plan, here is a list of 30 different content marketing tactics.

*Articles.* Using articles similar to those that would be found in a newspaper or magazine, article marketing includes the creation of content with the intention of distributing and syndicating it via various means, including article aggregator websites.

*Blogs.* Publishing original content using blog software, which organizes pages sequentially and/or categorically.

*Case studies.* Case studies are a written description that tells how a problem was successfully solved with a product or service.

*Digital newsletters.* These online newsletters are often published according to a schedule and regularly provide a source of useful information, promotion, and links to web pages that further engage readers.

*E-books.* Longer than a blog post or online article, an e-book provides a more in-depth analysis of a particular topic of expertise.

*E-mail.* From timed sequences of articles to special promotions, messages via e-mail continue to provide the highest conversion rates of any online marketing tactic.

*Images.* Content need not be overly verbose. Like the old saying, a picture is worth a thousand words—and sometimes a few thousand clicks.

*Infographics.* Just as the name implies, the field of infographics translates information, data, or knowledge into graphic visual representations. For example, why talk about percentages in the usual boring manner when a pie chart and textual facts can get the point across in a more interesting way?

*Microsites.* These types of websites are dedicated to specific campaigns or promotions. They may also be created to serve as a social hub for content that doesn't fit on the corporate website or blog.

*Mobile content.* Content and applications specifically created and formatted for mobile consumption are increasingly valuable in some markets.

*News releases.* Press release format, application, and distribution has changed so that press releases reach beyond journalists—they can be effective for directly appealing to consumers, too.

*PDFs.* Many of the types of content mentioned here, such as articles, case studies, white papers, and more, could be converted into PDFs and easily distributed.

*Podcasts.* Though not practical for all industries, audio files provide an effective promotion opportunity for some markets. Such audio files are often formatted as interviews, news reports, or infomercials. Like newsletters, podcasts are often distributed according to a schedule.

*Research.* Surveys, studies, research, and statistical data that provide insights can be very engaging and shareable. The information provided by them can work in tandem with many of the content types listed here.

*Slide shows*. Digital slide shows are often used to make presentations and pitches in person to make B2B sales, but they can
just as easily be uploaded to the Internet to appeal to a wider
audience.

*Social*. Content created exclusively for social networks like Facebook,
Twitter, or LinkedIn have significant impact on awareness and
engagement.

*Traditional media*. Content marketing can also be carried out through
traditional digital media, including newspapers, magazines, television, and radio.

*Videos*. Not everyone is engaged through reading or static imagery.
Some of the most engaging and rich content is in video format.

*Webinars*. One of the more advanced content marketing techniques
to be sure, webinars are audio combined with presentation slides,
often done in real time with a question-and-answer session and
the opportunity to chat. Once a webinar is finished and has been
recorded, it can be stored in an online archive for future audiences
to view.

*White papers*. White papers are used to educate readers and help people make decisions. These authoritative reports or guides dive deep
into a specific topic and can be very persuasive.

The mix of content types that you employ with your content plan is
really dependent on target customer preferences for content consumption,
your own resources for creation, and prioritization of content types for
their effectiveness. Consider not only the individual content object, but
also how content can work in a series such as a sequence of infographics or
articles, as well as in collaboration with other types of content and media
that are included in your overall marketing plan.

## HUB AND SPOKE PUBLISHING

With a diversity of content types and promotion channels, a hub and
spoke model for publishing can be very effective. The focal point provides a destination of organized content and media that can be ref-
erenced by customers, the media, or any other audience a brand is
after. Blogs are commonly used in a hub and spoke scenario since they
bridge the gap between corporate and conversational content so well.
(See Figure 8.3.)

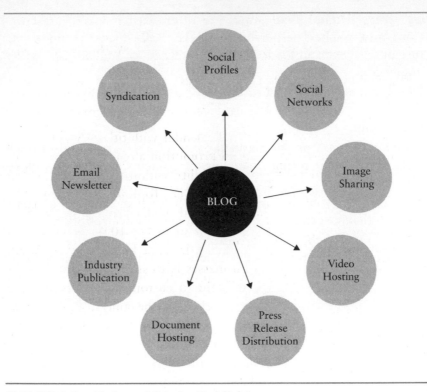

**FIGURE 8.3   Hub and Spoke Publishing**

For example, TopRank Online Marketing uses a blog (toprankblog .com) as a hub with spokes that serve as channels of distribution. When we publish a blog post, some of these channels are activated, and the blog post is promoted through them. In some cases, such as RSS and Twitter, it's automatic. In other cases, it depends on the media included in the blog post, such as videos which are promoted though YouTube as well as other video hosting services. Some of the promotion and content channels we use with blog marketing include:

- Facebook fan page
- Twitter
- Google+ page
- YouTube channel
- Flickr
- RSS

- RSS to e-mail (FeedBlitz)
- E-mail newsletters
- Guest blog posts
- Contributed articles to industry websites
- SlideShare

Our blog posts follow an editorial calendar with title, keywords, categories, tags, and methods of social promotion already defined. As we build out a keyword portfolio of visibility within search engines and the topics we're known for on the social web, TopRank's blog functions as the hub with spokes on various social media promotion channels that help to create an online footprint of an agency 10 times our size. If you're a small business, you can achieve the same kind of impact. What we recommend to many small businesses is to start with a hub like a blog and two or three spokes relevant to customer interests and the online communities where they spend time. As the company grows relationships, credibility, and savvy about content creation and social promotion, additional social spokes can be added.

## SOCIAL MEDIA SEO

A hub of content that promotes through social media channels and networks is the basis of many social media SEO tactics. This happens in a few different ways. First, when your social content (tweets, public Facebook updates, blog posts, YouTube videos, etc.) becomes keyword-optimized and attracts links from other websites, it will also attract natural search engine traffic.

In the case of Google it also helps that your Google+ brand page has been added to as many other Google+ circles as possible. As a result, when a search is performed on Google, the chances of your website content appearing in search results is much greater for those who have added your personal or brand Google+ account to their circles. How do you get others to add you or your brand to their circles? By creating and sharing useful content, commenting, plussing others' content and comments, and engaging with others on Google+.

The second way has to do with the fact that most social content is focused on specific topics. That's the nature of social media. It's about like-minded people connecting and sharing. When that content is keyword-optimized and easy to find in search by people who are actively looking, you can grow your social network simply by being easy to find and useful. Of course, when you promote the content through social spokes, the exposure to others might inspire some of them to link back to the source (your hub). Those links can send traffic and may also help Google and Bing decide your content is a great answer for what people are searching for. In other words, promoting useful and topically relevant content can attract links that help grow your social networks and improve your ranking on search engines.

The hub and spoke method of content organization and promotion can be applied and expanded in multiple ways for growing awareness of your brand, products, and services on search engines and within social networks. Better visibility on search engines and social networks isn't limited to marketing benefits, though. When journalists, analysts, and bloggers see your brand appear prominently on Google.com, Facebook, Yahoo! News, Bing, Twitter, as well as mentioned on prominent blogs, it will be clear that your business is an authority on the topic they're doing a story on. That's the kind of credibility that leads to media coverage. Authority, credibility, and influence are pretty important assets for businesses of all sizes, and when companies have great stories to tell, a hub and spoke publishing model can be instrumental in attracting and engaging communities of interest.

## CYCLE OF SOCIAL MEDIA AND SEO

A hub and spoke model of content publishing and promotion can only go so far based on internal company knowledge. When a company gains a certain amount of savvy with content, SEO, and social networking, it's important to develop a cyclical approach to improvement and growth. The cycle of social media and SEO is a method content marketers can use to develop and refine the effectiveness of their content with the customer segments it's meant for. The cycle is a feedback approach that can improve the relevancy and impact of your search optimization and social media promotion efforts. (See Figure 8.4.) The key is that the cycle should start with content. Here are the steps to developing your own cycle of social media and SEO insight.

1. *Creation.* With insight into customer personas, your keyword and social topic research guide a content marketing plan with a

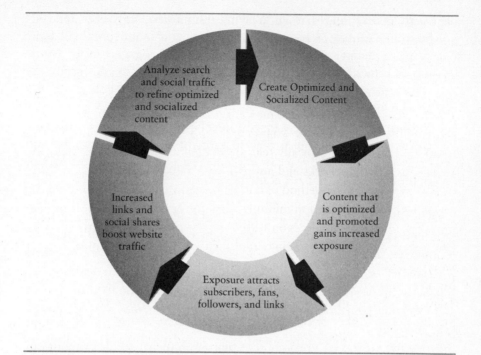

Analyze search and social traffic to refine optimized and socialized content

Create Optimized and Socialized Content

Content that is optimized and promoted gains increased exposure

Exposure attracts subscribers, fans, followers, and links

Increased links and social shares boost website traffic

**FIGURE 8.4    Cycle of Social Media and SEO**

component that's managed as a hub and spoke. Content is planned, optimized, and socially promoted to the communities of interest in your spokes around topics customers care about.

2. *Awareness.* As community members discover your optimized and socialized content, many will engage with it. They'll vote, share, comment, and discuss it. Some of those community members will be potential customers, some won't care at all, and some will be social influencers.

3. *Attraction.* With an optimized and socialized content plan that's committed to creating useful content relevant to customer needs, the community responds. The increased exposure of your content attracts more subscribers, fans, friends, followers, links, and visitors. You'll start to develop your own community.

4. *Growth.* With a growing reputation as a useful source of information, other websites and blogs respond. Increased links and social exposure increase your content's search rankings and referral traffic. There's a momentum growing that attracts visitors, fans, shares, and links with less promotion on your part.

5. *Analysis and insight.* With growing popularity, analysis of the traffic you've generated and the communities you've nurtured will assist in the refinement of future content and social engagement by focusing on topics and content formats that best resonate and inspire the community to engage. Engagement may be social shares; it could also be inquiries and sales.

6. *Repeat.* Armed with new insight into better-performing search keywords and social topics that inspire influential connections and community growth, you can implement an updated content plan of optimized and socialized content.

In this hyperconnected world, with fewer and fewer degrees of separation every day, it is important to recognize that your brand's network of influence does not stand alone. It is connected to a network of others who are tied to more still. Social influencers within relevant communities can cause ripples through the Internet, drawing attention to your content and elevating your brand's ranking in the search engines as more people visit and share.

Now that we have a great content plan with plenty of ideas about our audience and the role of content in reaching business goals, the next step in our journey involves striking a balance between content creation and curation.

## ACTION ITEMS

1. Take inventory of your current content assets, on and off of the company website.

2. Based on your research into customer segments, persona development, and keyword research, identify the types and formats of content that should be a part of your content plan.

3. Identify your hub (website, blog, microsite) and at least four potential distribution channels as spokes.

4. Develop a list of content types and messaging for your social networking and media sharing efforts.

5. Consider what other departments in your organization you could collaborate with in terms of content creation, optimization, and social promotion.

# CHAPTER 9

## Content Isn't King, It's the Kingdom: Creation and Curation

Google's executive chairman, Eric Schmidt, has been quoted as saying, "Every two days we now create as much information as we did from the dawn of civilization up until 2003."[1] That's a tremendous amount of content, and it represents the overload of information many online citizens experience between social networks, online news, e-mail, and entertainment. But content is what we do online. In fact, 53 percent of time spent on the Internet is directly attributable to content consumption.[2] Your prospective clients are consuming content every day. So are journalists, customers, job candidates, industry analysts, investors, and employees. The opportunity to connect with the communities that will help grow your business can be realized with a content marketing strategy that balances both curated and original content.

For an article on content curation, I reached out to a group of my peers who are experts in the content marketing arena and asked for their perspectives on the role of content curation. Here are some of their responses:

> Content curation, which can be defined as a highly proactive and selective approach to finding, collecting, presenting, and displaying digital content around predefined sets of criteria

and subject matter, has become essential to marketing, branding, journalism, reporting, and social media—often, to mash-ups of all these different and disparate channels.

*Rebecca Lieb, Digital Marketing and Media Analyst,*
*The Altimeter Group, and author of* **Content Marketing**

What is Expedia? It's an aggregation of airline and hotel feeds that then get aggregated to create content. What's Google? Google is an aggregation of a whole bunch of content. I'm a fan of doing that but the challenge is how can you do it in a way that's interesting? You have to make a decision: Do you let the machines do the aggregation and the selection or do you let humans do the selection. It's a huge decision, humans or machines.

*David Meerman Scott, Professional Keynote Speaker,*
*best-selling author of* **The New Rules of Marketing**
**and PR** *plus several other popular books*
*on digital marketing topics*

As more content floods through all aspects of the web (as well as print and online), we'll need more brands stepping up to make sense of what we really should be paying attention to. Content curation is as important in the content marketing toolbox as is creation. We need both.

*Joe Pulizzi, Founder of Junta42 and Content Marketing*
*Institute, coauthor of* **Get Content, Get Customers**
*and* **Managing Content Marketing**

Just a few years ago, audiences were starved for information and the role of media was to create it. Today, we are drowning in information and the emerging role for media is to filter and organize it. Marketers can build trust with their constituencies by providing focused curation in areas that matter to their constituents. Original content will always have value, but curation is coming to have nearly equal value.

*Paul Gillin, consultant, speaker, and author of*
*three books on social media marketing*

Most business marketers understand the notion of creating original content, although few feel confident about their ability to execute over prolonged periods of time. When I ask companies about their approach to content curation, I often hear a variety of explanations—and even more questions. Some of the most common questions companies ask about content marketing are answered by digging into the details of how creation and curation can work together. A few examples:

- With so many companies and individuals publishing content online, how do we stand out?
- How can we build thought leadership in our industry with prospects and the media?
- How can we gain SEO benefits efficiently?
- How can new content, along with useful resources we curate, fit within our online marketing mix?
- How do content creation and curation work best together to inspire customers to buy?

When I started blogging late in 2003, my passive objective, outside of learning about blogging as a communications and marketing platform, was to assemble interesting stories and add some of my own commentary. If you had asked me back then why I was blogging, my reply would have been something about building credibility and sharing industry news with staff and clients. Looking back, I was clearly curating content. Not just for friends, but for the online marketing industry at large. Through a combination of speaking events, curation, and original content, our agency was able to attract all of our new clients over the past 10 years without a sales team or buying advertising. (For a sample of our blog, see Figure 9.1.)

How did that happen? Over time, my descriptions of daily news on the blog became more in depth, and, while finding my blogging voice, I entered the world of content creation by writing articles. Those useful, keyword-optimized articles that demonstrated expertise and personality also attracted links, shares, and subscribers to our content, which led to clients like Hewlett-Packard, Marketo, and many other well known brands. Michael Brito, who was a search marketing manager at HP (and is now a senior vice president for social business planning at Edelman Digital), read, subscribed, and commented at TopRankBlog.com for more than six months before hiring our agency. He shared these kind

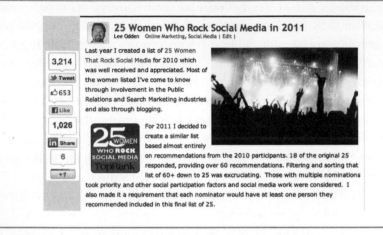

**FIGURE 9.1    25 Women Who Rock Social Media**

words about me and my blog: "Before I even met Lee, I truly knew his approach to search marketing because I read about it every day. I could see that he was at the top of his game" (Minneapolis *Star Tribune* 2007).

The "curation to creation" path I've described is pretty common among companies that are just starting out with a business blog. Depending on your goals and what customers need to know in order to buy from you, curation is a great starting point. How? I call it the "Oreo cookie tactic." Set up Google Alerts for a relevant topic and, when something piques your interest, take an excerpt of the article and write your own introduction and conclusion (with proper citation of the source, of course). Your contributions are the cookie part of the Oreo, and the excerpt is the white stuff in the middle. Blogging isn't the only platform for content curation, of course. In whatever ways ideas are being shared online, there's an opportunity to curate and create, to filter information and package it in a way that adds value.

A mix of creation and curation certainly worked for me and for many of the companies I've worked with over the past ten years. Will it work for you? That's what this chapter aims to answer.

## CREATION VERSUS CURATION

It's a bit of a silly question to ask, "Which is better, content creation or curation?" because there are clear benefits to each and for both together.

The optimized content marketing plan and editorial calendar you've created based on previous chapters should allow for original content creation where it can best facilitate your business objectives. The same guideline applies to content curation. Implement where it makes sense for your approach. My experience is that a mix of the two helps companies achieve a variety of online marketing objectives related to creating awareness, building thought leadership, and attracting new business through search and social media. Ann Handley, chief content officer of MarketingProfs agrees: "Mix curated content with original content, and don't rely on the curated stuff alone. Content curating is a perfectly good way to extend the content of your own site, but only 'in addition to' and not 'instead of' your original content."

To help you decide on the mix of curation and creation that's right for you, here are some of the common objectives for each.

### Content Curation Facilitates These Objectives

- Efficient, topically focused collection of information that appeals to customers looking for a "single source" on a particular topic.
- Grows awareness of your brand as a topical authority based on adding insight to industry commentary.
- Facilitates networking into spheres of influence in your industry. Collecting and sharing content from influential members of your community can get you on their radar, resulting in mentions, links, or even referrals.
- Attracts links from social sources like Facebook and Twitter. Social links can send traffic and influence social and standard search visibility.
- Attracts links from other websites, which can also send traffic and influence better visibility on search engines like Google and Bing.
- Keeps prospects engaged as part of your lead-nurturing efforts.

### Content Creation Facilitates These Objectives

- Builds thought leadership through original ideas and insights in your industry category.
- Communicates your brand's distinct voice, point of view, and personality in a format that you control.
- Facilitates storytelling about your brand's success in serving customers.
- Provides the material that facilitates movement of readers through your buying cycle based on your content plan.

- Attracts links from other relevant websites, blogs, and social networks to influence search and social media visibility.
- Provides a source of optimized content according to specific customer segments, keyword targets, and objectives.
- Creates source material for others to curate and share, including customers, prospects, employees, journalists, and industry bloggers.

What does a content curation and creation mix look like in action? Let's say our target persona is Sara, a purchasing manager for a chain of coffee shops that sells fair trade coffee and values doing business in an environmentally friendly way. For Sara, price is a factor, but she's also very eco-conscious about her suppliers and the products they offer. Through our research, we know that Sara's values and goals can be translated into search phrases like "recyclable coffee cups" and "eco-friendly coffee supplies." She's also interested in social topics via channels like blogs, Facebook, and niche forums such as "sustainability and coffee" and "easy to recycle."

With a basic understanding of what Sara cares about related to the products she needs to purchase, we can expand search keywords and social topics into a content plan that produces thoughtful, easy-to-find, and easy-to-share information that builds our brand awareness and credibility as a go-to source for environmentally conscious coffee shop supplies. Our content plan could involve curated content to build awareness such as collected news about environmental and fair trade issues related to the coffee industry as well as news about small business, retail business, and the geographic areas in which her company operates. Curated formats might include a news blog with RSS feed, an e-mail newsletter, and user-generated tips. Original content could include thought leadership articles from the CEO of the coffee shop supply company, articles about the company's advocacy of green commerce, and a series of answers to frequently asked questions about company products sourced from company sales and customer service personnel. Formats for original content might include a resource section about green coffee topics on the website, blog posts, images, and videos.

This combination of curated and original content will help attract and engage the Sara the Purchasing Manager through multiple touch points, including search engines and social networks. Consistency of message, community engagement, and relevant content that's easy to find on search engines and share on the social web will demonstrate that the coffee shop supply company has a business philosophy congruent with what Sara cares about. The company also demonstrates thought leadership and expertise by providing useful, curated industry news and specific, original stories related to its products and services in a helpful (versus "salesy") way.

## CONTENT SOURCING

Think about your customer personas and segments. As you review your content plan and what those customer groups care about relevant to your products and services, what types of content would resonate with your target customers? What words would they use to search? What topics would they discuss to find information on social networks? What would inspire them to engage, share, and buy? Keeping in mind what's relevant for the customer and brand relationship, here is a collection of content sources to consider:

- Engage with your community, and ideas will come out of those inter-actions. Look for common questions, misinformation to be clarified, and unique stories to share.
- Survey customers, blog subscribers, and social network members to find out concerns, their influences, and their goals.
- Look at popular questions on Quroa, Yahoo! Answers, and LinkedIn Answers relevant to your customer segments. Which questions are asked most often? Which questions are poorly answered that you can add value to?
- Mine your web analytics data for referring search keyword phrases that indicate common questions. Adding a filter by using words such as "how," "what," or "why" against the search phrases that delivered traffic to your website could indicate topics that interested customers seek answers to. Try a filter simply by using a "?" to see a broader range of questions that you might want to answer through new or curated content.
- If your website has an internal search engine, look at the search logs for the things visitors are searching for.
- Find out what frontline staffers (e.g., sales and customer service personnel) are being asked most often. This tactic is a gold mine for

finding the kind of information your customers are specifically looking for on the search and social web.

- Look at trending websites for seasonality or cyclicality in the
demand of search topics related to your products and services.
- Monitor stories in the news that match topics of interest to your customers (aka *newsjacking*) where your company could be a solution.
- Monitor competitors' names in social and traditional media for
opportunities to position your company as an alternative or to provide a counterpoint.
- Watch for industry reports, studies, and research that you can com-
pile and add commentary to.
- Analyze the content you've been publishing for effectiveness; expand the
things that are working and modify or reduce the areas that are not.

## CONTENT CURATION BEST PRACTICES

Blending a mix of new content with the filtering and management of other
useful information streams is a productive and manageable solution for providing prospective customers a steady stream of high-quality and relevant
content. There are several good services that facilitate curation tasks, such
as Curata, Curation Station, and CurationSoft. (See Figure 9.2.) Software

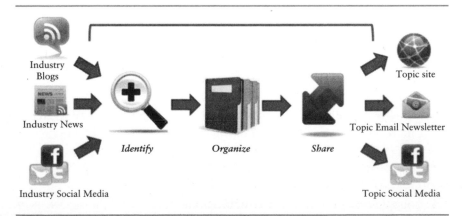

**FIGURE 9.2   Curata Content Creation Strategy**
Source: Curata.

can help, but on its own isn't the answer. Pure creation is demanding. Pure automation doesn't engage. Curating content can provide the best of both. Here are several best practices to help you with curation sources, types of content, and where to publish.

### Sources of News to Curate

- Industry-specific newsletters sent to you via e-mail
- Links to content and media shared on Twitter, Facebook, StumbleUpon, Reddit, and other social sharing websites
- Google Alerts, Google News, or Google+ Search
- Curation tools: Flipboard, Scoop.it, Storify.com
- Real-time search engines: Topsy, socialmention.com
- Niche topic blogs
- News aggregators: Alltop, popurls, Techmeme
- Bookmark and/or subscribe to updates from industry news, magazine, and blog websites
- Press release distribution services like PRWeb, PRNewswire, or Marketwire
- Monitoring competitor websites for mentions of their brand terms through Google Alerts and social media monitoring tools (e.g., Trackur or Radian6) to see what kind of curation tactics they're using

### Types of Content to Curate

- Useful resources relevant to your target audience: blogs, news, training, tips, networking, and industry events.
- Content created by influential people of importance to the target audience
- Statistics, research, and reports
- Compelling or provocative industry news
- Videos: YouTube, Vimeo, Viddler
- SlideShare presentations or search Google.com for .ppt file types
- White papers, e-books, and case studies
- Infographics and other data visualizations
- Tips, how-tos, and best practices
- Creating short lists of tips according to keyword themes

- Compiling large collections of resources according to topical theme
- Aggregating the best comments from other blogs or your own blog
- Running surveys, polls, and contests that result in content

**Where to Publish Curated Content**

- Company blogs
- E-books
- E-mail newsletters
- Social media channels
- Contributed articles or blog posts to industry sites
- Niche microsite dedicated to a specific news category

These are just a few suggestions, and the best ideas for content creation and curation will come from a specific analysis of your own customer groups and industry. The key is to do the homework of understanding what motivates your customers and to assemble a compelling mix of curated and original content to inspire them to engage and buy. Be thoughtful about the usefulness of the content you assemble, create, and promote. Empathize with your customers' interests and goals so you can properly optimize content for customers, search engines, and to inspire social media sharing.

It is my hope that these ideas have sparked your imagination for how you can leverage a mix of content creation and curation to build awareness and thought leadership for your brand, to attract links and traffic, and to stand out among the growing sea of online content. With a strong foundation of content marketing principles, now we can turn to leveraging our keyword research for best practices in content optimization and SEO copywriting.

**ACTION ITEMS**

1. What are your three most important objectives related to content marketing, and what role can content creation or curation play in your content marketing strategy to achieve them?
2. For which goals will you curate content? Which will require original content?

3. Identify 3 to 4 sources of content for curation. Start tracking topics relevant to your target audience and develop a process for identifying key topics for curation.

4. Set up Google Alerts or a special monitoring profile using your favorite social media monitoring tool for topics relevant to your audience and the business content marketing strategy. Find stories that you can use with the Oreo cookie approach to blogging and curation.

# CHAPTER 10

## If It Can Be Searched, It Can Be Optimized: Content Optimization

### SEO PAST AND PRESENT

In 1998, Google was a newly formed search engine created by Larry Page and Sergey Brin while they were at Stanford University. (See Figure 10.1.) Microsoft's Bing hadn't been thought of yet; Facebook certainly didn't exist; and other strange names filled the search engine marketplace, including AltaVista, Lycos, HotBot, and Excite. Only one name from those early days of search is still familiar today, and ironically, it didn't start out as a search engine, but as a directory: Yahoo!

Over the past 15 years the search engine world has changed dramatically. During that time, I have been an online marketing consultant, working with hundreds of clients, affecting thousands of websites, ranging from B2B start-ups to several Fortune 50 companies, and my experience has reinforced a single guiding principle: "Whatever can be searched, can be optimized."

The advent of social, universal, local, and personalized search has kept the state of SEO best practices in a state of flux. SEO consultants and search engines are involved in a continuing cat-and-mouse game of learning what it takes to improve positioning of web pages and other types of searchable, digital assets. In pursuit of every competitive advantage possible, marketers must understand that whatever content can

FIGURE 10.1    Google's Interface in 1998

be crawled, indexed, and sorted as a search result is an opportunity for optimization. Search engines are far from perfect, and the ability to facilitate search engine interaction with your website, when done correctly, can result in benefits that directly affect website visibility, traffic, and sales. For content marketers, it's particularly valuable to know that SEO can improve the visibility of many different types of documents and media, including web pages, images, video, PDF files, Microsoft Office documents, and a host of other file types, ranging from .swf to .txt.

Content marketing efforts can involve a range of content and media with specific audiences in mind. Being able to keyword-optimize articles, webinars, infographics, white papers, case studies, and more is a tremendous opportunity to connect brand messages with people who are actively looking through search.

## WHERE THERE'S SMOKE, THERE'S FIRE: CONTENT AND LINKS

Because of Google's PageRank algorithm, there's a symbiotic relationship between content, links and social media engagement for search visibility. Search engines use links to find and rank content. When great content is created, optimized, and socially shared online, it can attract links from other websites and exposure to new social networks. Those links attract visitors directly and can influence visibility on search engines, which can result in exposure that attracts even more links and social shares.

The advent of social media integration with search means the importance of external web page links as important "signals of credibility" for

> ⚇ Great job by +Brian Vellmure live logging my session on buying ...
> https://plus.google.com
> Lee Odden · Feb 7, 2012 · Public
> Great job by +Brian Vellmure live logging my session on buying cycle
> optimization (Search, Social & Content) at #OMS12
> ▪ Brian Vellmure shared this post:
> Integrating **Social, SEO** & Content - Online Marketing Summit 2012, San
> Diego, CA +Lee Odden Lee starts right in highlighting Google - what if Google
> disappeared ...

> ⚇ At the Intel Social Media Summit (Be Social) tomorrow I'm sharing ...
> https://plus.google.com
> Lee Odden · Jul 10, 2011 · Limited
> At the Intel Social Media Summit (Be Social) tomorrow I'm sharing newsrooms
> from Cisco, The Ford Story and of course the cool Free Press ...

**FIGURE 10.2    Google's Search Result for "Social SEO" Showing Google+ Social Shares by Brian Vellmure**

search engines has evolved to include social links. In addition to earn-ing and acquiring links from other websites, the links contained within social shares on sites like Facebook, Twitter, Pinterest, and especially Google+ can influence how customers are exposed to your brand in search results. (See Figure 10.2.)

Companies that have relied solely on SEO for attracting new business can no longer ignore the impact of social media content, promotion, and participation. We talk a lot more about link building and social promotion tactics in Chapter 12, but the relationship between optimized content, social media, and links should not be overlooked.

## FOR THE SEO WIN, GO HOLISTIC

Most organizations that produce a variety of different content types and search engines are doing their best to index that content so they can run ads next to it. Too *much* focus on SEO, and the content on high-ranking web pages may confuse readers, resulting in poor conversion rates. Too *little* focus on keywords can mean a lack of search engine traffic to your best content. Both situations should remind content marketers and copywriters to consider who their target audiences really are: search engines and customers.

### Cross-Channel Optimization

As companies realize they need to make their content more findable and socially interesting to reach and engage more customers, implementation is often a bit fragmented. For effective online marketing, it's important to promote a diversity of content according to the audience segments your company is after. That means promoting keyword optimization of content holistically and across channels. Well-executed keyword optimization is not only good for improving search visibility, but also for user experience by making it easy for consumers to find what they're looking for. Quality content optimization isn't about stuffing keywords in title tags and image alt text. It's about finding the right balance of keyword usage and effective copywriting that is helpful to both search engines and customers.

Good content marketing strategy calls for the development of purposeful content across the organization, including human resources, public relations, customer service, marketing, and sales. Content optimization for search and social media can be instrumental in helping that content become easier for intended audiences to find wherever they may be looking online. Individually, there's a benefit to each of those departmental content producers for improving search visibility of their content to target audiences. For example, by optimizing content, there will be more candidates in the hiring pipeline, more media inquiries from industry publications, more problems solved online (versus in call centers), and more inquiries, leads, and sales. Collectively, each of those departmental content producers can use SEO resources, such as shared keyword glossaries, relevant cross-linking, social content promotion, and coordinated content creation, to elevate overall brand search engine visibility.

If your online communications strategy calls for the company to become more authoritative and influential on broad industry topics, then web pages, company blog posts, guest posts on other blogs, contributed articles in industry publications, press releases, YouTube videos, tweets, Facebook status updates, public Google+ updates, and any other public content that can be discovered and crawled by a search engine is ripe for keyword optimization. Content SEO does not need to be limited to the content that lives on the corporate website or blog. The collective impact of marketing working together with public relations (PR), customer service, information technology (IT), human resources (HR), legal, marketing partners, business partners, resellers, dealer networks, distributors, affiliates, and other content producers can create a significant competitive advantage that would be extremely difficult for a competitor to duplicate.

### Phases of On-Page Content SEO

Resources, objectives, competitive situation, content management system, budget, and time frame all affect how optimization is implemented within a company. Here are three fairly common approaches to holistic on-page content SEO:

1. Core Optimization Audits: Conduct SEO audits of existing website content, including keyword research, technical SEO audit, content audit, social media audit, and link audit. SEO implementation is focused on optimization of current text, digital assets, and the content management system. Web analytics, monitoring, and Google/ Bing webmaster tools are enabled. Social profiles are created along with basic social sharing of content.

2. Priority Optimization: All five SEO audits are conducted, and SEO implementation is focused on current, priority content, such as products or services directed toward ideal customer personas that generate the most revenue or specific areas of business focus. New content and digital assets produced by various departments, including PR, HR, customer service, and marketing, follow SEO best practices. The content management system enables template-level technical SEO features. Ongoing monitoring of website search performance through web analytics and search engine webmaster tools allows refinement recommendations of content and technical SEO. Social network development and off-site social content creation work in concert with corporate content and website optimization efforts.

3. Comprehensive Optimization: Comprehensive SEO, social, and content marketing audits are completed. A content editorial plan is developed according to target customer segments and personas. Content producers within the organization are trained on SEO best practices. SEO best practices are also incorporated with the content creation processes of the organization and are made a consideration, with branding guidelines and style guides. Dynamic and targeted keyword glossaries are leveraged for long-term and on-demand optimized content creation. Community development with social networks facilitates content creation through crowdsourcing and user-generated content and also provides robust content promotion opportunity. Search, social media, and content marketing work in sync across the organization, guided by customer personas and corresponding content marketing strategy.

## LET'S GET OPTIMIZED: CONTENT, DIGITAL ASSETS, AND SOCIAL MEDIA OPTIMIZATION

Most companies think of text-based content optimization when the topic of SEO is discussed. With traditional SEO, web pages on the company website are evaluated for keyword presence based on a target list of researched phrases. Pages that are deemed relevant for a target keyword phrase are rewritten to provide more specific focus for the target topic that prospective customers are searching for. New pages are often created to complement existing content and optimization.

Within a content marketing plan, customer research leads to an identification of buyer interests and goals. Those customer preferences are synthesized into topics relevant to states in the buying funnel. From a broader perspective, topics can be mapped across the customer life cycle, from top of funnel awareness to supporting advocacy with existing customers. The topics identified as relevant to customer needs during their journey from awareness to consideration to purchase are the reference points for keyword research. Our optimization work with text content, digital assets, and some social media will be based on that keyword glossary.

According to the Content Marketing Institute's 2011 Content Marketing Playbook, the top 10 content marketing tactics in 2011 were:[1]

- Blogs
- E-newsletters
- White papers
- Articles
- E-books
- Case studies
- Testimonials
- Microblogging (i.e., Twitter)
- Webinars/webcasts
- Videos

The three types of content optimization we will cover are included on this list. Not only are these tactics effective on their own and as part of a content marketing strategy, but they can contribute to a more effective and holistic search engine optimization strategy.

## Content Optimization

Fundamental content optimization that extends beyond standard web pages can be applied to a variety of text-based content objects. Following are a few best practices for optimizing web pages and press releases, as well as useful SEO guidelines for other content marketing tactics, ranging from e-books to newsletters.

### Web Page Optimization

Most SEO efforts are focused on web pages. Effective web page optimization includes a consideration of the individual page as well as its relationship with other pages on the overall website. In your content plan, keywords are mapped to individual pages (for smaller sites) and to categories (for larger sites). Keyword association with web pages gives explicit guidelines on the page focus's relevance in regard to customers and search engines.

The notion of focus is very important with content optimization of any kind. Each web page or other content object that you're optimizing should have a singular, primary focus. That might mean you're optimizing each web page for anywhere from one to three keyword phrases. Any more than that, and you may dilute the effectiveness of your optimization efforts. If you try to cover too many topics with one web page, customers can become confused or distracted, leading to higher bounce rates.

The organization of pages and digital assets within a website, navigation, and anchor text links between pages affects how a search engine crawls the site. Think of a business organization chart with a CEO at the top, vice presidents underneath, and directors next, followed by managers and frontline employees. Putting content more than five directories deep in your website can give the impression that the fifth level content isn't very important. If your products and services content is buried that many levels deep, it might be difficult for people or search engines to conveniently find them. For example:

Too deep: domainname.com/level1/level2/level3/level4/level5/level6/
Ideal: domainname.com/category1/page1.php

Content should be easy to find through links between pages, and your most important web pages should be linked from your home page.

An HTML sitemap should offer links to all pages of a small site (fewer than 100 pages) and to the most important (or category) pages of a larger website. Other SEO considerations range from dealing with duplicate content to page speed to Google Webmaster Tools issues that would be covered in a technical SEO audit, which was described in Chapter 3.

### Keyword Placement

Here are some tips for placing a specific target keyword phrase to help a page be considered the most relevant answer for a topic:

- Title tag: Using 10 to 15 words, put the most important keywords first, followed by a compelling description. For example: Red Widgets—Best Prices, All Sizes & Free Shipping—Company XYZ.
- On-page title: Use the H1 attribute, "Red Widgets."
- Body copy: Use the exact-match target keyword phrase three to five times per 500 words or so. Variations and synonyms can be helpful for better copywriting. "Red Widgets," "Red Widget," "Widgets that are Red." Many SEO resources recommend at least 250 words on a web page in order for a page to rank well. It's important to have enough text for the page to stand out as an authoritative topic for the target keyword phrase. The search engine and your customers are after the "best answer," so if you expect to draw search engine traffic to a particular page, it should have enough content and media for a person to think exactly that. Search engines strive to anticipate human behaviors but are no more advanced than a five-year-old child, so we must help them by providing quality signals to use in determining the best content, just as we do with great copywriting for customers.
- Image alt text: "Red Widget." Be specific with the text and focus of the page.
- Anchor text links: "red widget." The text that links to another web page should be relevant to the destination. By association, the source page of the link will pass PageRank to the destination page, and the text used in the link will pass meaning. The flow of PageRank from one page to another through links is contingent on the link being "crawlable," a topic discussed further in Chapter 12.
- File name: Use separate descriptive, relevant keywords with a hyphen. For example:

  Best: www.domainname.com/keyword-category/keyword-product.php

Poor: www.domainname.com/cat_name/prod_name.php?id=
14kjnkk2j3b4bk23

- Social share: Programmed sharing widgets should automatically pull your keyword-optimized title tag or on-page title into the sharing form so that content is prefilled for the user along with the page URL. Make sharing easy by displaying appropriate widgets for social news and networking sites and you'll encourage more exposure to social communities and attract more social links. This is a fundamental feature of optimizing for search and for shares.

- SEO copywriting: Write for your customers first and foremost, but consider keywords as well. Use descriptive references instead of pronouns. Personal pronouns "I," "you," "she," "he," "it," "we," "you," and "they," and objective pronouns "me," "you," "her," "him," "it," "us," "you," and "them" have their place in great copy, but search-optimized content requires more descriptive references. For example, which one of the following phrases do you think is more descriptive and useful for both readers and search engines? (When you read optimized copy out loud, it should sound natural and interesting, not clumsy or awkward.)

"It is particularly effective when they use it with the products from company XYZ."

"Social media monitoring software from company 123 is particularly effective for social media strategists when used in combination with products from company XYZ."

- Meta description: While not a direct influence on rankings, keyword use and writing of the meta description tag is important for SEO effectiveness. Meta descriptions are short summaries of the web page and are often used by search engines to describe web pages that are included in search results. The more compelling and relevant your meta description is, the more likely it will inspire a click to the web page. More clicks mean more visitors, but also serve as a signal for potential influence on subsequent rankings. Pages that inspire more clicks may be rewarded with higher search visibility, because users are responding positively to them.

### Press Releases

One of the most effective methods of content distribution outside of e-mail, blogs, and social networks is through press release distribution. I started using PRWeb to promote content in press release format in 2001 and have seen numerous changes and challenges in the news distribution and news search space since. My agency has provided SEO consulting for more than five years to PRWeb, so we've had more front- and back-end exposure to what goes into effective press release optimization than most agencies working in online marketing.

Multiple studies have documented that consumers and journalists are actively searching for and reading press releases. Optimizing press releases for a specific audience makes them easier to find and therefore more of an asset for communicating news and attracting traffic to the company website. As a result, it makes sense for marketing and PR practitioners alike to understand how to make press release content easier to find through search and social media.

In addition to serving as a content distribution and discovery channel for PR and communications, optimized press releases can augment direct SEO link-building efforts. A well-written press release that includes embedded links to optimized web pages on the company site and that is distributed through a press release distribution service can be syndicated and copied as content on other news websites and blogs. When the links embedded in the release are retained in the copy hosted on a third-party news site or blog, they can serve as a link signal for search engines that can elevate search visibility of the page the links point to. In my 10-plus years' experience working with press release optimization and news search, a well-written press release that includes media such as images or video can attract anywhere from 50 to 500 inbound links from other websites. It's important to qualify this observation by noting that the press release, and media included in it, must be well written and relevant. Optimize for people first, then keywords.

Here's a checklist for best-practices press release SEO:

- Clearly define the goal and target audience of the release.
- Research relevant, popular keyword phrases (one or two per press release.)
- Add the target keyword phrases to the title, subheading, and body copy of the release.
- Use keyword phrases—not "click here"—when linking to landing pages or other corporate website pages.
- Add media to the release (images, video, audio) as well as alternative formats of the release (MS Word, PDF).
- To count conversions, use tracking codes in the URLs that point from the press release to landing pages.

- Post the release to the company's online newsroom.
- Write a blog post version of the announcement and include a link to the press release.
- Distribute the release via a wire service such as PRWeb, Marketwire, PRNewswire, or Business Wire.
- Optional: Create and distribute a social media version of the press release.
- Encourage bookmarking of press release pickups.
- Monitor release rankings, social mentions, traffic, and outcomes.

While it can increase visibility and link acquisition substantially, you don't have to distribute an optimized press release through a service like Marketwire, PRNewswire, Business Wire, or PRWeb. Many companies also post their press releases to a company newsroom. Publishing press releases to your own website offers some advantages, such as more control over formatting, placing keywords in the title tag, alt text, and the number of links to other pages on your website.

When archiving press releases on a company website, it's useful for journalists, consumers, and search engines if the releases are organized according to topic or keyword category and arranged chronologically. Many newsroom software solutions or blog software options like WordPress provide the opportunity to associate releases with both dates and topics as well as keyword tags for easier location by those visiting the newsroom. Newsrooms tend to host other media types, such as images and video, that can also be keyword-optimized for search. Press releases and news content optimization is not entirely different than web page optimization as far as keyword placement. What's important to understand is the audience you're after and how optimization efforts can positively affect visibility of your news content.

### Newsletters

Most companies publish some kind of e-mail newsletter. Depending on the format, the newsletter might contain all content within each e-mail file, or there may be landing pages involved. In either case, if the newsletter is open for public consumption and published online as web pages, it can be discoverable through search engines, becoming a valuable asset for overall SEO efforts.

Even if the information on past newsletters becomes outdated, it can still be a useful asset for search-based discovery. If the published date of the newsletter page is past a certain point in time, a pop-up window can be programmed to appear instructing the reader to subscribe and visit the main newsletter index. Alternatively, the archived newsletters might use formatting in the header that displays a prominent message guiding visitors to the main newsletter index for the newest content. Old content can be modified to present messages to users that guide them to an index. In this way, each archived document retains the link equity acquired over time and continues to attract search traffic without alienating readers with old information.

The same keyword placement guidelines for a web page apply to any other HTML-based document. For newsletters, think about which keyword topics and structures would be relevant for the content now and in the future. Use those keyword expressions in the title tag, on-page title, image alt text, body copy, and as anchor text from the newsletter to landing pages or other pages of the company website. Many email newsletters use tracking codes in links that point externally. You might consider removing those tracking URLs for the web version of your newsletter so that links are "clean" and crawlable by search engine bots.

The newsletter index should offer a list of past newsletters with links and descriptions to each issue. A simple list of links using dates as anchor text isn't very SEO- or consumer-friendly. A chronological archive of past newsletters is somewhat useful, but a categorical archive is more effective for letting readers and search engines understand where to go for information on specific topics.

Furthermore, repurposing newsletter content allows you to gain even more SEO value. It really depends on how the newsletter is structured. In your content marketing plan, let's say that each newsletter will include a particular tip of 150 to 250 words. These tips follow the interests of your customer personas, content plan, and the corresponding keywords. If the newsletter is monthly or weekly, the tips from each edition could be compiled into one post on the company blog or used in an incentive fulfillment piece to attract future subscribers.

These SEO best practices for newsletters apply to any type of company content that follows a particular format and schedule for publishing, including white papers, e-books, research, and reports.

### White Papers and E-books

White papers and e-books are often placed behind a registration form as a PDF document, so most companies don't feel the need to optimize them for search or social sharing. However, you can employ several tactics to provide more promotion value for the white papers or e-books while creating an asset for search and social media discovery at the same time.

Executive summaries are the low-hanging fruit needed to create public content for a white paper or e-book. This content can live on the landing page or as a supplement in PDF format. PDF files can include keyword-rich titles and text as well as embedded links back to the landing page or topically relevant pages on the company website. Social sharing links or icons are also useful for PDF files to make it easy for readers to point friends on social networks to the page.

Summary text could be customized for each customer segment and therefore keyword-optimized for the topics that are most relevant for those specific customer interests and goals. Different areas of the white paper, e-book, or report could be summarized or rewritten in blog post format to provide relevant diversity. In order to add more customization to the summaries or promotional blog posts, key personnel associated with the content could be interviewed on video to be used as complementary content. In addition to being embedded on the summary or landing page, the videos could be uploaded to YouTube or other video hosting services, optimized, and shared through social channels with a link back. When content objects used as part of a content marketing program are viewed as modular or as individual components, a wide range of content repurposing opportunities becomes possible.

### Case Studies and Testimonials

Case studies and testimonials are powerful assets for storytelling and inspiring confidence. They are also extremely useful opportunities for optimizing and socializing content designed to attract, engage and inspire specific customer segments. When planning content for case studies and testimonials, think of the topics that your target customer groups care about. Those topics should influence the themes of your case studies as well as the questions you put to customers when in search of endorsements. A classic SEO tactic for optimizing interviews is to use keywords in the interview questions to inspire answers that support the target keyword topic. As with other collections, an index page that includes keyword-rich titles as links along with useful descriptions will help both search engines and readers understand what you have to offer and where to find it.

In-depth case studies usually include other media, such as images and, in some cases, video. We get into some specifics of optimizing these types of digital assets next, but it's important to be aware of all possible content objects that can serve as potential entry points through search into your website. The target audience for a case study isn't limited to potential customers. Journalists, bloggers, industry analysts, and marketing partners might look for examples of your company in action, too. Regardless of the audience for your case studies or testimonials, making the text, image, and video content search- and social media–friendly can improve visibility, traffic, and attention to your most important brand stories.

### Digital Asset Optimization

Before 2007, search engine results pages were made up almost entirely of web pages. If you wanted to find images, blogs, news, or video, you would need to visit a search engine specific to that media type. Then came universal search. Cited by Search Engine Land's Danny Sullivan as "the most radical change to [Google's] search results ever," this new effort at creating a more relevant experience for searchers involved bringing more data or media assets into the search results from the main search box. In addition to web pages, your search might also include results from Google's news, video, images, local, and book search engines.

The SEO community began assessing the diversity of content types and sources that could make up the search experience for target keywords. The different digital assets that could now appear in search results meant SEO professionals needed to start paying more attention to how search engines ranked a variety of file types, because each could potentially become an entry point to the website being marketed. The concept of holistic SEO existed before this, but with the variety of content and file types appearing in search results, it became important to step back and look at the bigger picture of the user search experience. Since that time, Google has throttled down somewhat on the frequency of news, video, images, local, and books appearing in search results, but they still represent a significant opportunity for top visibility on important search terms. The practice of optimizing for these media types is something I described as "digital asset optimization" in 2007 and has been known as such ever since. (See Figure 10.3.)

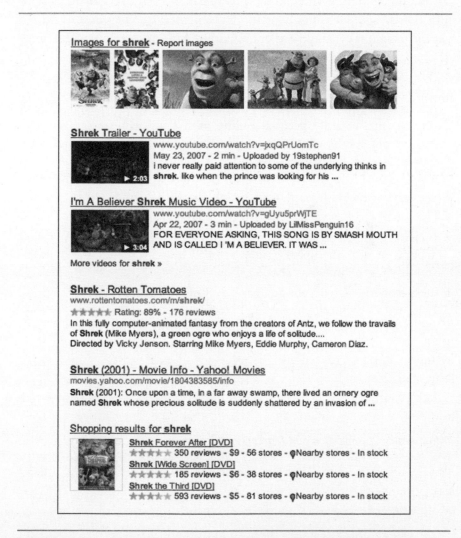

**FIGURE 10.3    DAO Search Engine Results Page (SERP) Shrek**

*Images*

Among the most common digital assets for optimization are images. Images are also a commonly shared social media object. Image hosting and social sharing site Flickr hosts more than 6 billion images, and traffic to social image sharing site Pinterest grew over 4,000 percent in the last six months of 2011. Images can be discovered through specific search engines or appear within universal search results for certain queries. Within the content marketing mix, images are often overlooked as optimization assets, since most content marketing tends to emphasize text. To get the most out of images for optimization, here are a few essential tips:

- Find the right images: There are many guidelines for image use online, especially when it comes to copyright. As much as possible, use images you own or have purchased outright. Royalty-free stock photos can certainly be used online with your website or blog and can serve as optimization assets, but they may be used by other companies as well. Images with use governed by Creative Commons must also be considered carefully to comply with the owner's specifications.
- Use keywords in file names, such as keyword1-keyword2.jpg.
- Use a focused keyword phrase in the image alt text.
- Include a description or caption along with the image. Any text around or near the image might be used by search engines to understand what the image is about.
- Text embedded with the image may not be read by search engines. Even with advancements in OCR technology, search engine bots are not currently able to effectively understand text within images.
- Don't stuff keywords into image file names, alt text, or captions. The notion of focus applies to optimization of any kind of content, so overuse can cause confusion or dilution. Be specific with your keyword optimization and you'll stand out from other, similar content.

*Infographics Optimization and Marketing*

Infographic images have grown significantly in popularity. Data visualization can be very powerful, and with that popularity comes attention. Even though it can be argued that infographics are overused, quality infographics continue to produce significant results in terms of attention, traffic, and link acquisition. To get the most out of an investment in infographics for marketing and promotion, consider these 11 tips:

1. Involve credible sources in the data collection, such as prominent companies, people, or research organizations, and then encourage those sources to help you promote the resulting graphic.
2. Create a blog post for the infographic and support promotion of it through the blog's social channels such as Facebook, Twitter, Google+, e-mail, Reddit, or StumbleUpon.
3. Segment the infographic into modular pieces that can be used in blog posts and shared on image hosting sites like Flickr, with links back to the main page that hosts the full infographic. A week or two after publishing and promoting the infographic, upload the full image and unique description to Flickr, with a link back to the original web page.
4. Schedule tweets of specific data points mentioned in the infographic over time with a link back to the full infographic. Keep in mind that 10 data points or statistics equals 10 tweets, and if you have more than one Twitter account, you might cross-promote those tweets. A similar, but more conservative, approach can work with Facebook as well.
5. Submit the infographic to aggregators and directories. Here is a short list:

   http://dailyinfographic.com/

   www.coolinfographics.com/

   www.infographicsshowcase.com/

   http://submitinfographics.com/

   www.infographicsarchive.com/

   www.visual.ly/

   http://infographicjournal.com/

6. Promote the infographic with a partial embed within an article or news release that also includes a link to the full infographic. Distribute the news release through a press release distribution service.
7. Highlight the infographic in an e-mail promotion to your in-house prospect or customer list. Include a segment of the graphic and a link for readers to see the full image on your website or blog.
8. Pitch relevant industry bloggers and media on the story behind the data included in the infographic. Focus on relevant, personalized e-mails and offer previews or prerelease opportunities for more influential sources.

9. Share the infographic with influential users of social news and bookmarking sites such as StumbleUpon, Pinterest, Delicious, or Reddit. You might also enlist a connected social media marketing service to do it for you.
10. Create a screencast video explaining the infographic and promote it through YouTube and other video hosting services.
11. Deconstruct the infographic into a PowerPoint and PDF document to be shared on SlideShare, Scribd, Docstoc, and other document hosting services.

Of course, all of these repurposed uses of the infographic should consider the use of relevant keywords for optimization. Make sure the infographic file name includes relevant keywords as well as the text on the web page used to describe the infographic. Social sharing buttons on the page that hosts the infographic should be easy to see and use. Include a text area form element with code that users can copy to embed the infographic, with a link back to your site, on their own website or blog to increase link traffic and improve search visibility.

### Video

With more than 600 videos being uploaded to YouTube every 60 seconds, the popularity of online video has reached epic proportions. Videos are effective for all markets and types of customers, from B2C to B2B, small businesses and large. If your customer research reveals preferences for content consumption in a video format, there are many opportunities to optimize for discovery where those customers are looking.

My friend Greg Jarboe, who has written a book on video optimization titled *YouTube and Video Marketing: An Hour a Day*, offers these essential tips on video marketing and SEO:

> YouTube SEO involves including keywords in the title, description and tags. Attracting views and ratings is also helpful for better rankings on YouTube. Web video SEO involves using keywords on the page the video is embedded in as well as in anchor text links to the page. Filenames, metadata and RSS enclosures are also opportunities for keyword inclusion.

Along with Greg's tips, here are a few essential video optimization guidelines relevant to YouTube and other video hosting services that you can use to improve search visibility and engagement for your video content.

1. As with any other type of content, video SEO involves optimizing with relevant keywords, both for search engines and for user experience. Use keywords in the raw file name, title, tags, URL, and link text to the video page. Beyond that, include a paragraph of optimized text that provides a brief description of the video. The benefits of text in association with video are twofold: user experience and search visibility. This is important, because interaction and engagement with a video can influence its ranking in conjunction with relevant keywords.

2. Optimize your channel page. Video hosting and sharing sites like YouTube and Vimeo are effective tools for gaining visibility. Video hosting services offer opportunities to optimize individual videos as well as a channel page, which serves as a sort of index to your uploaded videos. Use keywords in naming the channel and in the description, and be thoughtful of which site you link to.

3. Encourage viewers to interact with and share your videos. The fundamental success principle for video content that gets shared is to create content that's actually worth sharing! If your video isn't interesting, relevant, entertaining, or informative, viewers aren't likely to share it, let alone view it. You'll also want to encourage viewers to comment on the video and make it easy for users to share on their favorite social networks. YouTube provides built-in sharing options, but if the video is embedded on your company website or blog, then include a sharing widget.

4. Repurpose your videos. You can extend the value of your investment in video creation as well as reach by repurposing video content. The embed feature offered by video hosting services makes it easy for others to publish your videos on other websites. Consider that possibility as you create video content. As you create video content, consider experimenting with short and long videos. Use teaser videos of one to two minutes to attract attention and that link to longer, more in-depth videos. Here are some other repurposing tactics for video:

   o Use transcriptions of videos to create blog posts or content for web pages.

   o Take screen shots from videos and post them to Flickr and other image-sharing sites.

o Turn offline content, such as training videos or videos of a conference keynote speech, into optimized digital assets for your website.

Treat video optimization as you would other types of content that have been developed to meet customer needs through your brand's content and solutions. Consider how your target audience or personas prefer to consume content like video. Where do they find and share video? What topics are they interested in relevant to the products and services you offer? How will video help you tell the stories that will inspire viewers to take action (e.g., to seek more information, to buy, and/or to share)?

### PDF and MS Office Documents

One of the most common file formats for content marketing tactics is PDF. Companies also post Microsoft Office documents such as MS Word, Excel, and PowerPoint online fairly frequently. All of these document types can be crawled and ranked by search engines. And you know what that means: What can be searched can be optimized!

Best-practices SEO for PDF and Microsoft Office documents is consistent with what I've described for web pages, newsletters, and case studies. Use relevant keywords in file names and in the copy within the documents. If you use templates to create PDFs and MS Word documents, then make sure the template logo links to your company home page. Include a keyword-rich tagline in the footer, and link relevant text from that tagline to an appropriate page on your website. When appropriate for the kind of content you're publishing, include links to social sharing options like Facebook, Twitter, Google+, and others that are important to your target audience.

If you host a collection of PDF files, then create an index with keywords used in the titles that link to the actual files. Also include short descriptions next to each document title. The same guidelines apply if you manage collections of MS Word docs, PowerPoint files, and Excel spreadsheets.

## Social Media Optimization

As we've moved through content and digital asset optimization, you've probably noticed a pattern. Find out what customers care about, what that means in terms of keywords, and then create or optimize content so it's easy to find when people search those keywords. This basic process applies holistically to any kind of online content, as that pattern will help you see the value and opportunities of optimizing social media.

What follows next is a description of how you can apply SEO best practices to content and platforms that are inherently social. Keyword-optimized social content makes it easier for people to find by using search. Promoting keyword-optimized web content and digital assets through social channels exposes that content to a community empowered to share and to link. Those shares and links can send traffic and serve as signals that search engines use to position your content in the search results.

### Blogs

Blogs are one of the most powerful publishing platforms that integrate the best of SEO, content marketing, and social media optimization. Comments, social shares, and integration with offsite social websites create compelling opportunities to engage readers and build a community. Blog software such as WordPress makes it incredibly easy to organize content in a search- and social media–friendly way. From the blog name and tagline to categories, post titles, and tags, there are abundant opportunities to provide readers and search engines with clear signals on what your content is all about.

Effective business blogging requires a commitment and a plan. After personally blogging for more than eight years, I can tell you it has been both challenging and rewarding, with the benefits far outweighing the costs in time and effort. Not only has blogging and search visibility of our agency blog resulted in numerous consulting engagements, speaking gigs, media coverage, and new employees, but it has led me to writing this book. Making it easy to discover your blog content through search and social media can have an incredible impact on your business, just as it did with mine.

Since keywords represent our attempt to empathize with customer interests through stories about our solutions, here's a hit list for keyword placement with blogging. You'll notice some similarities with some of the optimization principles we discussed earlier in the chapter.

- Blog name: It's more important to have a memorable blog name than a keyword-rich blog name. If you can do both, it's a bonus.

- Blog tagline: This text may be very similar to your meta description tag and offers a good opportunity to use the most important keyword phrase that is relevant for your the overall blog.
- Logo alt text: The name of your blog, or the single most important keyword phrase, is appropriate here.
- Post titles: Blog post title tags should be written for search engines using the most important keyword first. The on-page title should be written for readers and to inspire social shares. For example,

  Title Tag: Kindle Fire Cases: 5 Reviews of Leather, Fabric & Plastic Cases for the Kindle Fire

  On-page Title: All New Kindle Fire Case Reviews! Find Out Which One Was Rated the Best.
- Categories: Going by the top-level topics and target keywords in your content plan, create relevantly named categories.
- Body copy: Going by your content plan, write blog posts intentionally designed to focus on specific topics. You may want to use a more free-form style for train-of-thought posts, but consider the topics of interest to your target audience. Use keywords as a guide, not a mandate, for blog writing. In the end, your blog posts should not look "optimized," just clear and easy to understand. Remember, you're writing and optimizing for customers first, then search engines.
- Lists: Sidebar lists of other blogs, popular posts, popular comments, and similar information can be helpful for adding keyword representation to your template.
- Anchor text links: Use keywords when linking from one blog post to another. If the post you're writing links to another web page or a previous blog post, the text used in that link should reflect the topic of the destination. For example, a blog post about widgets that links to another post about red widgets should use "red widgets" as the anchor text. If the page about red widgets is properly optimized, it will use "red widgets" in the title tag, on-page title, image alt text, and body copy.
- Tags: Not all blogs use tags. Some use categories instead of tags and some use tags in addition to categories. Tags represent a folksonomy of content organization for finding past blog posts. The usefulness of tags essentially equates to keywords. If a category of "widget reviews" is selected, the more specific "fabric widgets," "leather widgets," and "plastic widgets" might be the appropriate tags to use.

- Image alt text: Including images with a blog post is almost always a good idea. Images are powerful metaphors or complements to the text content and can also provide an opportunity to optimize. Alt text for an image should be specific to the image or to the most important keyword phrase for the blog post. Focus on specifics, and do not "stuff" multiple phrases or you'll simply dilute the impact.

The social media optimization aspect of blogs involves adding sharing widgets to the blog template that makes it easy for readers to share your content with social networks relevant to your target audience and the communities that influence them. Most blogs use sharing widgets from Facebook, LinkedIn, Google+, and Twitter. Some might also include StumbleUpon. Many of the social sharing widgets that blogs use include counters. The social proof of numerous "likes" or shares of a post can help tentative readers decide to read your blog post and may even contribute to their motivation for sharing.

Pay attention to the topics and blog post formats that tend to do well in social media channels of interest to your target audience. Learn from those that attract substantial social shares, comments, and links. Be willing to adjust your formats to better accommodate the content consumption preferences of those with whom you're trying to connect. For example, you might start out with image-rich content and discover your readers want longer-form text content.

Create a keyword matrix for your blog content plan that will help you plan content at least three to six months in advance with flexibility for wildcard or spontaneous topics. Follow a schedule each week, such as Monday Thought Leadership, Wednesday Practical Tips, and Friday Weekly Industry News. Consider keywords and your customer personas with this schedule and also take advantage of current events and topics to respond to. Provide something of value that readers cannot find elsewhere while making your blog content easy to find in search engines and a popular topic on social networks.

### Twitter

You can do many things on Twitter to create and share content beyond individual tweets. Engaging with followers by asking and answering questions can turn into many great content ideas. Since virtually all Twitter content is public, things like Twitter chats are a great way to create searchable content and to connect with like-minded communities. Curating a Twitter chat into a blog post or by using Storify is an effective way to crowdsource content.

As for specific SEO tips on Twitter, public tweets that include keywords and links can provide useful signals for search engines that can increase the reach of your brand messages. Here are some of the areas within Twitter where you can use keywords to improve search visibility of your tweets.

- Twitter real name: This is a user name of up to 20 characters.
- Twitter handle: Use @companyname or @companynamekeyword.
- Twitter profile description: You have 160 characters to work with. Make it count. Including @ Twitter handles will convert them to links. You can also include full URLs that will become clickable. These links will include the no-follow attribute, so they will not pass PageRank. That's okay, because including links to make it easy to visit your website means you're optimizing for customers.
- Twitter profile photo: Use keywords in the file name of the image.
- Tweets: Although 140 characters doesn't seem like a lot, being succinct in your messages and including links is a great exercise in building interest. Use a social media content plan to guide the topics you pick to share content about.
- Hashtags: These are most commonly used with Twitter chats like the fine #blogchat Mack Collier runs on Sunday nights at 8 p.m. central time. They're also used like tags or keywords to add context to a tweet.
- Twitter lists: Name your list using relevant keywords, and assemble the A-team for each topic you'd like to cover.
- Write tweets that are short, to the point, and leave room to be retweeted.
- Use a URL shortener, such as bit.ly, that 301 redirects (i.e., a code meaning "moved permanently"). This will help pass PageRank to what you are linking to and can also offer basic analytics information on how your shortened links are interacted with.
- Share images and videos within Twitter to attract more engagement with followers.

Social media optimization is as much about optimizing for sharing and engagement with the community as it is for improving search visibility. It comes down to understanding how your customer personas and those who influence them use the platform. As part of your hub and spoke content promotion model, Twitter can be very useful for promoting optimized content to those empowered to pass it on and link. The links within Twitter might not pass PageRank, but when Twitter users who become aware of your useful content through Twitter decide to link from their website or blog, those links are often ideal signals for better search engine visibility.

### Facebook

Because most Facebook content that users interact with requires a log-in to see, Facebook optimization efforts can affect visibility of content in several unique ways, specifically within the news feed and Facebook content that appears in public search engines like Google and Bing. Here are tips for improving visibility of your content in each of those situations.

- Facebook News Feed: When your news feed is set to show Highlighted Stories First, the "objects" that your network has shared with you (links, photos, updates) are sorted according to interactions with the content that has been shared, the affinity of the object creator and the person viewing it, and how long it's been since the object was created. You can optimize your brand's news feed by inspiring your Facebook fans and network to interact with the content you share. Basically, that means sharing interesting content. Post images and videos, interact with fans, ask questions, link to useful content, and offer timely, relevant information. Be engaging, tie in to current events, and, even though it's useful to follow your social media content plan, find ways to be spontaneous. Recognize those who interact with your content to inspire even more. The key to news feed optimization isn't the number of fans a brand has, but the quality of interactions the brand has with those fans.

- Public Facebook content on Google and Bing: Optimizing public content on Facebook for better search visibility is not unlike optimizing a web page. The difference is that you only have control over certain parts of the page to add relevant keyword content. The name of your fan page is one consideration, although this is the brand name that will represent you across Facebook. Do you want to be known as "Red Widgets," as "Company XYZ," or as some combination thereof (e.g., "Company XYZ Widgets")? Use keywords in your About and Info tabs as well as with image file names and titles of videos that you upload to attract links from other websites and blogs to your fan page. Also consider cross-linking to your Facebook fan page from other social profiles and blogs that you manage, such as Google+. If you are building a new fan page, you'll be able to secure a vanity URL after the page has 25 likes. The vanity URL can include keywords relevant to your primary topic of focus. When publishing an individual fan page update, use the text area for a keyword-inspired message. When linking to another website, Facebook will autofill the title and description from the site you're linking to. Those can be edited by putting your cursor in those areas and clicking to edit. The "Write Something" field is another opportunity for keyword-optimized content when you publish a fan page update. Fan page Notes could be used to create bloglike content on your fan page. Technically, Notes can appear within public search results where the title of the Note becomes the title tag of the page.

Facebook is a fast-changing environment for creating content, engaging with fans, and finding opportunities to include keyword-rich content in a relevant way. As a dynamic platform, it's entirely possible that the SEO value of some of these recommendations will change over time. As with your other social media participation, Facebook activity should be guided by a content plan that allows for keyword-optimized content beyond the initial setup of the fan page into the individual content that is shared through updates.

### LinkedIn

As with Facebook, much of LinkedIn content is behind a log-in. Individual users can make some or all of their LinkedIn profile content public and available to search engines, including Summary, Experience, Skills (aka keywords) and Websites and Interests (more keywords). LinkedIn group administrators can also make all of a group's content public (for search engines to find) or private. For companies that want to leverage their employees' LinkedIn participation for the benefit of the brand, suggestions to consistently use the employer's company name, along with adding links to the company website and blog, are reasonable requests. Individuals can employ apps that could syndicate external content from blog posts, Twitter, SlideShare, and a variety of other applications.

LinkedIn Company Pages offer several opportunities to add public content and therefore keywords for improved search visibility on search engines like Google, Yahoo!, or Bing.

- Company description: You have 461 characters to share a summary about your company, which can include separate paragraphs but no other formatting.
- Website: Link to your company website.
- Updates: With 379 characters to work with, updates are like a long tweet. You can include links to outside web pages, which behaves much the same as on Facebook. The autofilled description can be edited. Only designated administrators can publish updates.
- Syndicate company blog posts: The RSS feed of your company blog can be provided, and LinkedIn will post the headline and date.
- Careers: Paid job listings will appear, but no descriptive text until you click through on the link. Job listings are time-sensitive and expire.
- Products and services: Here you can add product or service name, image, description, key features, website address, special promotions, a disclaimer, and video content. Individual products and services have their own web page and can be recommended by LinkedIn members.

Internally, LinkedIn for an individual member behaves very similarly to Twitter or Facebook, allowing users to post updates with links and media and for other users to interact with and share those updates. Posts from Twitter or a blog can be automatically posted to a user's LinkedIn updates. There are many categories of search within LinkedIn, including people, updates, jobs, companies, answers, your in-box, skills, expertise, and groups.

### Google+

One of the newest entrants to major social networks is Google+, and there are a number of ways that content within Google+ can become an SEO asset on Google.com. The incorporation of Google+ voting widgets on websites all over the web provides Google with a tremendous amount of information that could be used as a ranking signal for individual content objects or media. When logged in, Google users view web pages in the search results that their friends have Googled. Google has made it as easy to "plus" on the web as it is to "like" in the world of

Facebook. The content optimization opportunities with Google+ can be divided between individual users pages and brand pages. Here are several Google+ optimization tips that you can implement.

- Individual Google+ pages: Content areas of SEO opportunity include a tagline under your name, an introduction that offers rich formatting options and links, "bragging rights," and occupation. There are also fields for links to your other social profiles, other websites that you contribute to, and recommended links. You can upload photos and videos that offer the opportunity to write descriptions using relevant keywords. You can also capture and share short videos directly within Google+. Besides being able to upload images and videos directly, posts can be added, along with a robust amount of text. Links can be shared outside of the post, and Google+ will autofill the title and description without the option to edit. You can use your own name for an individual Google+ account or a pseudonym. Google+ allows you to add links to your other social profiles, places where you contribute as an author, and custom links such as your company website, blog, and other favorite websites you want to be associated with. Validated Google+ accounts that cross link per Google specifications between Google+ profile and external websites the author contributes to can result in the author's Google+ profile avatar appearing in search results. Such an enhancement to a search result listing can make a page stand out significantly from other pages, even if they rank higher.
- Brand Google+ pages: The name used with your brand page can be what you want. As with personal pages, there is a tagline field under the name where you can use keywords in the description. The introduction offers the same rich formatting, and there are fields for phone number and website. Link categories are limited to Recommended links. Images and video can be uploaded along with descriptions. Posts behave the same way as personal Google+ pages, with the option to share text alone or in combination with a link, image, or video. Both personal and brand pages offer the option to create video Hangouts.

All sharing options within Google+ offer control over level of exposure, whether it's to a specific circle of friends or the public web. Google+ is still very new and expected to achieve well over 100 million users in 2012. Many more changes are in store that will allow Google to further integrate Google+ explicitly into search and that will add features to personal and brand pages. As with all social media marketing platforms, active use and monitoring will reveal changes in the platform that require modification of content marketing approach or tactics. This is the way of SEO and social media marketing: Plan, implement, adapt, and refine. Repeat.

We've covered a lot of ground in this chapter! I hope you now have a good understanding of optimization as something that extends far beyond SEO for products and services. An optimized state of mind will enable you to see the "optimize and socialize" opportunities with any kind of content or media published online. If your customers are searching for or socializing about a topic relevant to your business, then optimization will help ensure that you're visible and part of the conversation. Despite all our good efforts with best-practices content optimization, it is but the yin to the link-building and content-promotion yang. Luckily, we cover exactly what that means in Chapter 11.

## ACTION ITEMS

1. Take inventory of your current content assets, on and off the corporate website. Identify SEO and social media audit opportunities for each type and category of content.
2. Map your target keywords to existing website and social media content for phase 1 optimization.
3. Compare your target keyword lists to the content and digital assets you have. Identify the gaps as opportunities for new content and media creation.
4. Review your content plan and identify which content types and digital assets you'll need to optimize for specific keywords on a go forward.

# CHAPTER 11

## Community Rules: Social Network Development

### *Don't Be Late to the Social Networking Party*

A friend recently asked me a compelling question about social media marketing for an article he was writing: "How long does it take to see any kind of ROI from a social media marketing campaign?" The answer to that question is an appropriate introduction to this chapter, because it reveals the importance of growing a social network as well as investing in relationships and community through social channels.

If a business like Brian Clark's Copyblogger Media announced a new software product through a series of demonstration videos promoted on the main web site to the Copyblogger community, via e-mail, and through social channels like Facebook and Twitter, I'd estimate that it would take a few hours to a few days before significant orders started coming in. Why so fast? Brian, Sonia, and their team have already built a hub and numerous spokes as social networks. The Copyblogger Media brand is known among buyers and numerous online marketing influentials as a provider of quality software. Brian has committed to creating content and media for several years, building up a strong online presence and attracting thousands of links and top search visibility on Google and Bing. With those online and offline social connections, search visibility, and credibility in place, barriers to conversion for a new product launch are low.

Now let's take another perspective. At a recent event, I talked with a small business owner who was lamenting about not updating his website and also that his competition was showing up "all over the place" online. The nature of his product requires some education and suffers from a few common misperceptions. The rapid advancements in technology of his particular product category are not very well known among his target consumer market. However, there's a substantial amount of search volume and interest on social networks in the solutions provided by his product. This is a classic scenario involving a small business owner with limited time and budget. Having limited resources calls for content, optimization, and clever social promotion. One way to approach the situation might involve a blog and videos of the business owner talking about his prospects' most frequently asked questions and showcasing implementations of his product. Providing answers though video would certainly engage prospects and inspire links and social shares. Except . . . how would anyone know that his great video content exists? Without a social network in place or an advertising budget, it could take this business weeks or months before they begin attracting significant sales.

The time to start building social networks isn't when you need them. The time to start is long beforehand, because it takes time to develop relationships. It takes time to listen, participate, create optimized content, and understand which triggers will inspire sales and referrals. If the small business owner mentioned here stays the course—creating useful content, listening to customer feedback, and growing a social presence—he'll not only increase his ability to reach a larger, relevant audience, but he'll also be able to tap into a steady stream of new content ideas, customer referrals, and channels of content distribution that can reach even more prospective customers. With a healthy social network and community, he'll have new channels for sharing optimized content that attracts links and social shares, essential signals for search engines to rank web pages that will drive even more new customers to his business.

## A PRACTICAL APPROACH TO SOCIAL NETWORK DEVELOPMENT

Earlier, we talked about understanding what our customers care about and where they spend their time on the social web. Publishing optimized content is only part of the puzzle when you are trying to attract and engage customers and influence them to buy. If customers are spending time on Facebook talking about topics relevant to your business, then by all means you should develop a social presence on Facebook. If customers subscribe and engage by commenting on certain blogs, forums, or LinkedIn groups, then those destinations are candidates for your participation as well.

Increasingly, customers are becoming more sophisticated about their use of online tools, from grandmothers joining Facebook to President Obama joining Instagram. Consumers are also spending more time with multiple social networks and may even transition from one network to the next, as many people have moved from MySpace to Facebook or Facebook to Google+. In order to attract, engage, and inspire your customers, it's important for brands to have relevant visibility where their customers are. To do that, you must determine where conversations are happening relevant to your products-and-services. In Chapter 3 we talked about implementing a social media listening effort to identify social topics and social channels relevant to your customers' interests. Now we'll take that information and work on growing the spokes of our content distribution channels with social network development.

## WHERE TO START WITH SOCIAL?

Many companies go after the most popular social networks with a "fish where the fish are" approach. That's not an unreasonable strategy, but it's a lot like putting up a billboard on a popular highway. What if your customers don't drive down that highway?

Choosing a social network based on popularity alone is not effective. Why? Because relevancy rules on the social web. The social media monitoring, surveys, and customer research we talked about in the planning phase will give you the insight into which specific social networks are most likely to reach and engage your customers and connect with industry influencers. At the same time, since there are a handful of social networks that capture the vast majority of consumer attention, the chances that one or more of them would be relevant for your online marketing strategy is pretty good. When that's the case, we need to look beyond the popularity of the network and also consider how best to use it for our purposes.

## CUSTOMERS ARE NOT YOUR ONLY SOCIAL AUDIENCE

A big part of effective content marketing isn't just about having well-written and compelling content. You must be able to get that content in front of customers who care, as well as people who are influential and can pass it along to their networks. Your approach to social networking should be thoughtful about the customers you wish to engage directly, as well as the influencers who may not necessarily be your buyers, but can help spread the good word about all of that great content you've been creating. Forrester Analyst Augie Ray breaks social influencers into three categories, each with varying degrees of influence:[1]

1. Social broadcasters (at the top)
2. Mass influencers (middle)
3. Potential influencers (bottom of the pyramid)

Of the influencers listed, the potential influencers make up 84 percent of the population, so it makes sense to consider that broad audience in the long-tail portion of your content plan. Connecting with social influencers at any level can extend the reach of your optimized content to attract links, shares, and new customers.

## THE ROLE OF "BRANDIVIDUALS" AND BRANDS

"Brandividuals" is a term coined by David Armano to describe individuals who represent a company brand as well as their own. Most brandividuals are viewed as online brand advocates, but the notion of personal brand and growing a network to promote a business is not a new concept. For as long as there has been word of mouth and sales made by referral, there have been individuals growing their networks to promote products and services. Today, there are simply new tools like social networks to make the connections and foster relationships.

There are many modern-day brandividuals, but one who stands out is the head of social media at Ford, Scott Monty. I've known Scott online for several years, and we've connected in person at many different conferences. On a trip with my son Cameron to Dearborn, Michigan, in 2010, we visited with Scott at Ford's world headquarters. My son was enamored with the story and history of Henry Ford, so Scott arranged a tour of the Henry Ford Museum and the Rouge truck factory. I've always been impressed with Scott's work as a social media advocate and he's been instrumental as a driving force behind Ford's success with social media.

Being able to learn and subsequently blog about the history of this more-than-a-century-old company through experiences at the Henry Ford Museum and sitting down with Bob Kreipke, Ford's full-time historian, was priceless. Without social networking, neither the visit nor my blogging about the experience on one of the most popular marketing blogs on the Internet would have happened.

Compared to the stories we heard about Henry Ford and Thomas Edison from Bob Kreipke, Ford is a very different company today, as is the automotive industry. It's not enough just to be innovative, but now you need to be able to innovate quickly and connect with customers in more meaningful ways. Based on my discussions with Scott, Ford is very committed to making those connections. Over the years, Ford has benefited from the broad reach that Scott's brandividualism has been able to provide. Many skeptics have argued that Scott was putting himself before the brand by using his name as his Twitter handle and using a photo of himself for the profile. However, Scott has in fact put a face behind a large corporation, which has allowed him to have more personal and "real" connections with followers.

If people are active in their industry by engaging, sharing opinions, and promoting themselves and their own ideas, it can result in awareness and growth of a social network. The outcome of becoming known and talked about by others is a personal brand: what you stand for, what your expertise is, and what you're known for. That personal brand can have a direct effect on the business brand the individual represents, and vice versa.

In an increasingly social world of business, consumers and buyers want to connect with people (versus corporate voices). That means investing in developing content, relationships, and engagement between

### Why do customers connect with brands on social networks?[2]

- They are looking for deals or discounts.
- They love the brand and want to follow it.
- They want to keep up with brand news.
- They noticed someone else following the brand/company profile.
- Others in their social network recommended it.
- An ad (print, TV, online) led them to it.
- It was mentioned in an article.
- They have a professional interest.
- The company's tweets/posts are entertaining.

Source: eMarketer 2011

individuals working for a company and the people they want to do business with. The ease of publishing and the popularity of social networks means that working with brandividuals, either as employees or as influencers in your market, is inevitable. The key for brands that want to leverage brandividuals for network growth is to have clear goals, a vision for what the brand stands for, and relevant communications. The effect can be a mutually beneficial outcome that recognizes the individual's contribution and inspires company credibility among a new or broader social network.

## THE BIG FIVE SOCIAL NETWORKS

In the hub and spoke model we've discussed for content marketing and social promotion, the hub is surrounded by a constellation of social networks and channels of distribution. Promoting optimized content through social channels can attract visitors, social engagement, shares, and links. Many online marketers believe that social signals are increasingly important for SEO.[3] Therefore, it's important to understand the opportunities for social promotion of optimized content. (See Figure 11.1.)

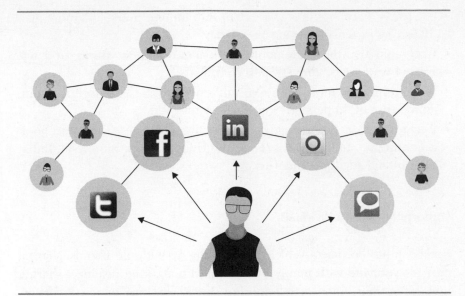

**FIGURE 11.1    Social Network Development**

Within the context of a content marketing strategy, my recommended approach to growing social networks is based on finding the most relevant places that your customers and influencers spend their time. Because popular social networks and media sharing sites represent the vast majority of social networking activity online, this chapter provides an overview, as well as opportunities for individuals and for companies, for content marketing on each of the top five.

All social networks offer various advertising opportunities, which can also facilitate network growth, customer engagement and even revenue outcomes. Our focus on social networks for this book is on the organic and content marketing opportunities, so I'll leave Facebook advertising advice to experts like Marty Weintrab and his book, *Killer Facebook Ads*.

## FACEBOOK

When you mention social networks or even social media, one of the first brands that comes to mind is Facebook, which started on the Harvard campus in 2004 and is now worldwide. The transformation that Facebook has made over the past eight years is nothing less than astounding.

- Currently, Facebook has more than 800 million users, and more than 50 percent of active users log in each day.[4]
- Every minute, there are more than 695,000 new status updates, 79,364 wall posts, and 510,040 comments.[5]
- In March 2011, more than 690 million visitors used Facebook.com, an increase of 43 percent over the previous year.[6]
- According to a recent study, the top five countries using Facebook according to number of users are: the United States, Indonesia, India, the United Kingdom, and Turkey.[7]

### Opportunities for Individuals

Facebook has become a vehicle for catching up with old friends, sharing parts of your life with family or friends who are long distance, sharing updates of your mood or relationship status, checking in at your favorite restaurant, and having the ability to "like" groups, pages, or brands. Many groups of friends use Facebook to coordinate get-togethers like parties or even weddings. For well-known business professionals, authors, sports figures, and celebrities, personal fan pages create an opportunity to grow and engage with social networks separate from personal pages on Facebook.

The content publishing and sharing opportunities on Facebook range from 60,000-character status updates to photos and videos. The Timeline feature, enabled for all users late in 2011, provides far more historical information on individuals than any other social network. Individuals are currently limited to networks of 5,000 "friends" or "likes" of Business pages, but individual Profiles can migrate to a Business page, which offers far greater limits.

### Opportunities for Brands and Organizations

The application of Facebook for business has become somewhat of a focal point of many online marketing campaigns. Utilizing Facebook as part of a marketing strategy enables companies to:

- Facilitate one-to-one, one-to-many, or many-to-many conversations
- Build connections and relationships with individuals

- Listen to what brand fans are interested in
- Create and cross-promote shareable content
- Offer promotions and special offers
- Interact with current and potential customers

An example of a company that has taken Facebook marketing to the next level is Obeo, a virtual tour and professional photography company out of Salt Lake City, Utah. (See Figure 11.2.) Obeo has taken a

**FIGURE 11.2 Obeo's Facebook Company Page**

very interactive and visually appealing approach, which offers special deals for liking its page, easy sign-ups for demonstrations, recognition of top fans, and weekly trivia to encourage users to return to its page frequently.

Facebook Business or Fan Pages provide a variety of content promotion opportunities using text, images, videos, and applications (apps). Social network growth for brands on Facebook is multifaceted, including content and promotions within Facebook, the ability to integrate Facebook "likes," and the capability to embed social widgets and commenting functionality on external web pages and offline promotions. Businesses with successful Facebook presence promote their Facebook Business Fan Page everywhere they promote the company website. Along with promotion is the ability to deliver on the brand promise of being useful for customers by publishing useful, timely, and relevant content.

## YOUTUBE

YouTube was launched in 2005 by three former PayPal employees, Chad Hurley, Steve Chen, and Jawed Karim, and sold only 21 months later for an estimated $1.65 billion to Google.[8, 9] Video as a platform is one of the most engaging forms of any social media. If a picture is worth a thousand words, then a video could be worth millions. Many people don't think of YouTube as a social network or even a search engine, yet YouTube has been ranked second only to Google as a search engine.[10] YouTube's social networking features allow users to connect with other video publishers and viewers. With hundreds of millions of users, YouTube is one of the largest social networks online.

- Within a year of launching, YouTube had more than 65,000 videos available and 20 million unique users per month.[11]
- More than 24 hours of video is uploaded to YouTube every minute.[12]
- An estimated 27.9 million men, 34.7 million women, and 21.6 million teens interact with YouTube on a regular basis.[13]
- YouTube's user base spans 25 countries and 43 languages.[14]
- YouTube averages 800 million unique user visits each month.[15]

## Opportunities for Individuals

YouTube has been the launching point for the careers of many popular musicians and pop culture icons, including teen sensation Justin Bieber. YouTube has shown us the best and the worst of the human race—from entertaining Internet sensations like Ray William Johnson, with more than 5 million subscribers, and iJustine, with more than a million subscribers, to the stupid and sometimes very painful mistakes made by amateur daredevils. Using intuitive online tools, individuals can create their own channels to upload and publish video content. YouTube provides users with the ability to interact with videos and video publishers through subscribing, rating, and sharing with external social networks. Videos can also be embedded on external websites. With a built-in social network, YouTube is an attractive option for individuals to promote content and grow their social networks both on and off of YouTube.

## Opportunities for Brands and Organizations

YouTube has proven to be a great platform for consumer brands: Orabrush, Blendtec, and Old Spice have gained millions of views and increased sales. In 2009, bottled water company Evian published a video called "Roller Babies," with US and international versions of the video viewed more than 68 million times.[16] (See Figure 11.3.) B2B brands have also succeeded; for example, Cisco has more than 10,000 YouTube channel subscribers, and "The Future of Shopping" video has more than 6.5 million views.[17] Creative, useful, and entertaining videos for B2C and B2B audiences inspire sharing among the YouTube community as well as with off-site social networks. Companies can leverage video in their content marketing mix, not only to reach customers with a more engaging format, but also to attract subscribers who complement an overall social network community. Optimized video hosted with YouTube helps video discovery through search engines like Google and on YouTube's own internal search engine. As new viewers discover a business video channel or individual videos, the network of subscribers will grow, creating a larger community to consume and share.

**FIGURE 11.3**   **Evian Roller Baby YouTube Video**

## TWITTER

The 2006 launch of Twitter introduced the concept of *microblogging* (short, 140-character messages known as *tweets*) to the masses. After news of natural disasters, political events, and celebrities entered the Twittersphere. The simplicity of Twitter and its ease of use on any device, from computer to tablet to smartphone, have enabled millions of people to connect, share, and engage through short messages. Videos and images can also be shared on Twitter. While many companies grapple with the usefulness and even return on investment of a 140-character message, successful online marketers have learned that the cumulative effect of sharing tweets can grow an active audience waiting to see what will be shared next. Twitter content is public and has been used by Google in the past to influence social search visibility.

- In 2011, Twitter reached 100 million active users.[18]
- Twitter usage on mobile devices has increased by 187 percent in the past year.[19]

- A record of 8,868 tweets per second was reached on August 28, 2011.[20]
- The tweet that was retweeted the most in 2011 was a tweet promoted by Wendy's that raised $50,000 for foster children.[21]
- A mere 5 percent of users create 75 percent of Twitter content.[22]

### Opportunities for Individuals

The top 10 followed Twitter accounts are not brands but celebrities. Twitter has become a great resource for sharing your passions, finding a job, and interacting with friends and industry peers. The sharing of news items has replaced the RSS feed for many Twitter users as a way to stay on top of what's new and current. In some cases, individuals have achieved larger networks than the brands they work for on Twitter. For example, web-hosting provider Rackspace has about 20,000 followers on Twitter, but brandividual employee Robert Scoble has more than 230,000 followers. Individuals can grow their networks on Twitter by promoting useful, timely, and well-written tweets and by connecting with other influential Twitter users who will retweet their messages. As with other social network environments, blatant self-promotion on Twitter is frowned on.

### Opportunities for Brands and Organizations

Twitter's built-in search functionality makes it easier for brands and organizations to target prospective clients more efficiently. Another great use of Twitter Search is finding your competitors and observing how they use Twitter and with whom they're connecting. As I've mentioned in earlier chapters, Twitter chats are also a great opportunity for experts within your organization to answer questions for prospective customers in real time. I've participated in numerous Twitter chats on marketing, SEO, and social media topics and have experienced firsthand how chats on Twitter can achieve a substantial reach. In fact, in late October of 2011, I participated as a guest on Mack Collier's #blogchat, talking about how to live-blog conferences in advance of BlogWorld

Expo. Our chat had more than 800 participants, 4,000 tweets, and 29 million impressions.[23]

Another example of effective Twitter use involves Curtis Kimball, who began selling crème brûlée from a food cart in the Mission District of San Francisco in 2009. At the time, the crème brûlée cart was not licensed, so his only way of communicating with potential customers was through the use of social networking sites like Facebook and Twitter. After only a few years, the Creme Brulee Man has more than 20,000 followers on Twitter. Curtis continues to use his Twitter account as a means of letting consumers know where he will be on a daily basis. What started as a small, meager cart has now become a thriving catering and food cart business in the heart of San Francisco.

Promoting useful content and engaging with your network is the most effective way to grow a network on Twitter. As a communications and networking channel, Twitter can be a news source, a syndication channel for blog posts, a cross-promotion tool for Facebook, and a way to survey or poll your community for ideas. For companies that have been successful with Twitter, the tactics mentioned can be useful in these ways and more.

## LINKEDIN

Shortly after social networking sites like Friendster and MySpace were created, the founders of LinkedIn saw an opportunity to create a business-centric site for users to connect with and nurture the relationships of business contacts. In a 2006 interview with *Businessweek*, cofounder Konstantin Guericke differentiated LinkedIn from other networks by saying, "We're here to build a business, not to create something cool. MySpace and Facebook have done really well. And I think they can monetize what they have built, probably by adding in more e-commerce. But I think the opportunity on the business side is ultimately larger."[24] Since its inception, LinkedIn has seen a steady growth rate and continues to expand its worldwide reach.

- LinkedIn was created in 2002 in the living room of cofounder Reid Hoffman.[25]
- As of November 2011, LinkedIn had more than 135 million members in more than 200 countries and territories, making it the third largest professional network on the Internet today.[26]

## Opportunities for Individuals

LinkedIn has proven to be an essential platform for individuals to nurture relationships with existing contacts, search for employment, and interact with particular brands and organizations. LinkedIn has also enabled individuals to establish themselves as subject matter experts and participate within groups as well as in question-and-answer forums. LinkedIn is a popular next step to connect with people after exchanging business cards at conferences and business meetings. Individuals can grow their network by searching LinkedIn for others with similar professional interests and by participating in Groups and Answers.

## Opportunities for Brands and Organizations

LinkedIn's search capabilities provide a great means of connecting with the right contacts at the companies that you would like as clients. For instance, say that you are looking to sign up a new digital marketing client at large corporation and are interested in contacting the vice president of marketing. LinkedIn will show you how many degrees of separation exist between you and that vice president, as well as which contacts you may have in common. By working your way up the list, you can facilitate an introduction to the VP without coming off as overly aggressive. Because LinkedIn is a professional networking tool, the recruiting options are very robust. There are special upgrades that recruiters or hiring managers can purchase to make finding candidates even easier. LinkedIn company pages are a great avenue for sharing content about your company, its products and services, recruiting new employees, and sharing information about your team.

## GOOGLE+

The launch of Google's most successful venture into the social networking space has proven to be much more successful than its previous social networking and sharing endeavors such as Google Wave and Google Buzz. Does Google+ offer a secret sauce for improved search engine optimization? Some sources have said that utilizing Google's +1 button can increase searchability for some sites, but not all, while other SEO pundits claim that the +1 button dramatically increases visits. There's a bit of an anticipated network effect with Google+. The more users that Google can encourage or incentivize people to use Google+, the more effective it will be as a social network and as a signal of influence on search engine rankings.

- Google+ launched in June of 2011.
- Websites using Google's +1 button get 3.5 times more visits than Google+.[27]
- In December of 2011, Google+ passed 62 million users and is estimated to reach 400 million by the end of 2012.[28]

### Opportunities for Individuals

One of the interesting features about Google+ is the ability to separate contacts into different "circles" and share content within those selected circles. This feature has made it easier to interact differently with family, friends, or professional contacts. Video hangouts can be live-streamed and saved to YouTube as part of a content creation and social engagement strategy. Content, images, and video shared publicly on Google+ can appear on Google.com search results within a short period of time. Growing a social network on Google+ involves "plusing" others' content, leaving comments, and adding others to your own circles. The "plus" is akin to Facebook's "like" and has become just as ubiquitous on the web, with implementation on thousands of websites. The more of your friends that add you to their Google+ circles, the more often content you share and publish will appear in their search results.

### Opportunities for Brands and Organizations

With much anticipation and a little controversy, Google launched an option for brands called Google+ Pages. Many of the same features found on individual accounts can be found on Google+ Pages, including the ability to post updates, upload images and videos, segment those followed into circles, and interact with others' content. Google+ Hangouts enable interaction with loyal fans through video. Practical applications of Hangouts for B2B organizations might include video-conferencing to answer questions, conduct training, or hold creative pitches. Not surprisingly, at the time of writing this book, Google brands occupy many of the top 10 brands on Google+, including Android, Google Chrome, Google+, Google, and Gmail. Other top brands on Google+ include H&M, the *New York Times*, and Marvel Comics.[29] Most brands participating with Google+ Pages are working to find the proper mix of activity, content sharing, and engagement to build substantial communities. Like many new social networks, many brands will attract fans based on previous social network participation in other channels. Since Google+ is so integrated with Google search results, and both paid and organic search results can be "plused," brands have every incentive to leverage content promotion and network growth. The more people who have added a brand to their Google+ Circles, the greater the chance that brand will appear in those users' Google search results.

## THE SOCIAL NETWORKING PARTY IS JUST GETTING STARTED

Forrester's Digital Marketing forecast for 2011 to 2016 predicts that social network investment will increase 300 percent over the next five years.[30] The intersection of social content, media sharing, and networking with search, e-mail, and even online advertising has made it an indispensable part of any effective online marketing strategy. Companies that invest in building social networks, develop communities of brand advocates, and offer social media–friendly content will have substantial advantages over competitors that wait until the day they actually need those networks before beginning to develop them. It takes time to build relationships and meaningful connections. The more comfortable a company can become with social tools for both marketing and internal collaboration, the more empowered the organization will be at succeeding on the search and social web.

## ACTION ITEMS

1. Identify which social networks fit best with your target customer objectives.

2. In which social networks do you already have a presence? In which will you start?

3. Determine which social networks you can use to cross-promote and repurpose content.

4. Identify key influencers within each social channel you'll be participating in and decide how you plan on engaging with them.

# CHAPTER 12

## Electrify Your Content: Promotion and Link Building

One of the guiding principles behind an "optimize and socialize" approach to content marketing is the impact of content discovery: If it can be searched, it can be optimized. If it can be found, it can be shared. Part of our understanding about customers comes from the topics that are of interest to them, which we synthesize into social topics and search keywords. Content plans incorporate those topics and keywords into information and media that will guide prospects through the sales funnel to purchase, share, and refer. The missing link with great content is that it isn't great unless people can find it. That's where content promotion, outreach, and link building come into play.

In the world of search engine optimization, links from relevant websites to your content have traditionally been one of the most significant external influences on how web pages were sorted in search results. The incorporation of social signals, such as content and links shared within social channels, has augmented web-page-to-web-page links in a significant way. For example, Google has made a number of changes, including the tighter integration of Google+, into search results through its social search initiatives and the addition of its new Personal Search option, "Search plus Your World," which draws content from your network on Google as well as content from the web at large.[1] Promoting content to your network on Google+ can result in more "pluses" of your content, which can influence the ranking of that content for users who are logged in to any Google service.

The tighter integration between Google users' social network content with the search engine experience means content publishing, promotion, and networking on Google+ is essential for companies that expect to be found in Google search. For context, imagine the hub and spoke content publishing model we discussed earlier with Google+ as a spoke. Content published on the hub can be promoted on the various spokes, or distribution channels, in order to increase visibility to end consumers, to influencers who may further promote the content to their networks, and to those who are prone to share and link.

For example, on a daily basis we publish blog posts on www.toprankblog .com as part of our content marketing strategy. Each topically focused blog post is automatically syndicated through an RSS feed created by our blog software, WordPress. That feed is shared with various syndication services, as well as more than 46,000 people who have subscribed to the feed. At the same time, each blog post is automatically promoted to the 16,000 people following the @TopRank Twitter account using TwitterFeed. Another automatic promotion channel for the blog involves RSS to e-mail through a service called FeedBlitz, which reaches more than 4,000 additional subscribers. Automatic promotion of content through social channels is something to be careful of. Use it too much, and readers will see your activity as overly aggressive. If you promote too little or not at all, your content may be missed in the mass of content being shared every second on the social web. (See Figure 12.1.)

Along with automatic promotion of content, there is manual promotion and outreach. Continuing with our own best practices as a walk-the-talk online marketing agency, the blog posts on toprankblog. com leverage the social networks we participate in, such as Facebook, personal Twitter accounts, LinkedIn, and Google+. According to what we know to be effective and important to our target audience, titles, descriptions, and timing of promotion will vary according to the social channel. Twitter promotions can use tools like Timely or Buffer, which analyze your Twitter network's tendency to retweet, and schedule the publishing of your tweets in such a way as to maximize the likelihood of sharing. That tactic can promote blog posts, public Google+ and Facebook posts, YouTube videos, or any other type of public social media content.

Other manual promotions of blog content are dependent on the type of media. If a YouTube video, an infographic, or a SlideShare presentation is embedded in a blog post, then any third-party syndication or reposting of that media can link directly back to the original. A number of image hosting services, including Flickr, Picasa, and Pinterest, provide additional channels for image promotion. The same is true with video hosting services outside of YouTube, such as Vimeo or Viddler, which can help promote your video content to new audiences. The mix of promotion channels depends on the content, your intent, and the nature of the communities that you'll be sharing content with.

With content promotion and social sharing, it's important to build trust and credibility among the community of members so that they will interact with and share your content. If your content promotion approach focuses solely on your own material, then you may quickly be designated a social narcissist and blatant self-promoter. The percentages can vary, but a 70 percent mix of third-party content combined with 30 percent of your own is a good ratio. Obviously, this can vary according to social

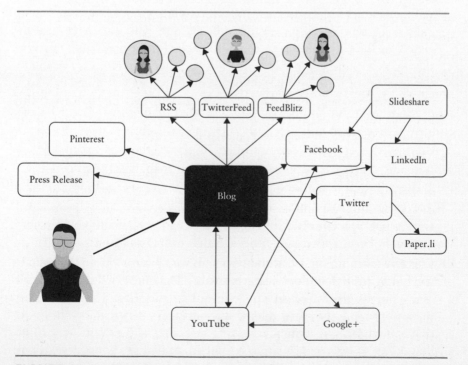

**FIGURE 12.1   Blog Promotion Channels**

channel and your reason for participation. Personal accounts may lean closer to 20 percent self-promotion, whereas brand social accounts are expected to share their own material and may approach 40 percent self-promotion. You'll need to determine through firsthand experience what the best mix is for your purposes and adjust accordingly. As a starting point, you can't go wrong sharing useful third-party content first.

Along with automatic and manual social content promotion is social outreach. Content promotion objectives include exposure to end consumers, influencers, and people who are authors themselves and link to interesting things discovered online. Outreach can be a very effective method of gaining exposure and links from highly influential people, blogs, and publications in your industry. Known as *online media relations* or *social media PR*, the practice of cultivating a list of industry movers and shakers with powerful social networks requires intelligent homework, patience, and creativity. Here are a few tips on researching, romancing, and engaging with influencers for outreach with a particular emphasis on Twitter, blogs, and journalists:

- With a channel like Twitter, use followerwonk.com or klout.com to find individuals who focus on certain subjects and who also have healthy networks. To find journalists, use muckrack.com or lists maintained by specific newspapers or publications like nytimes.com/twitter. The qualitative aspect of an individuals influence needs to be determined by direct observation of their social network activity. Do they get retweeted (by humans) often? Do they stay on topic? Do they communicate in a credible way? Will they respond to you or follow you back?

- Making a connection through any other social network should emphasize being useful. With Twitter, start by following and even making a Twitter list of those you'd like to engage with. Retweet their messages, and respond to their tweets on occasion in a meaningful way. Once you are followed back, you can send a direct message, although if you are creative, public requests can work just as well.

- Effective pitching on social networks and media for outreach, including blogs, must focus on being relevant. That means the people you reach out to should be directly relevant to the topic you're promoting and prone to tweeting, blogging, sharing, or writing articles about that same topic. Promoting gray-area relevancy is a surefire way to be ignored or to become known as a "flack," as bad pitch media relations pros are called in the public relations world.

- Blogger outreach is something I try to do every day. For 15 minutes each morning, I look at a selection of bookmarked news websites for stories on which I can make meaningful comments. Those comments link back to my blog or Facebook account, depending on the comment management service. I also look at top news for targeted topics in Google News or other newswire services to find relevant stories on platforms that allow comments or the ability to e-mail the author. In a number of cases, the comments I've made were called out or positioned above others, "sticky post" style, which was even more desirable than being mentioned in the article, since I controlled the content being presented without any editing.

- As you develop connections with influential members of the community and industry, your ability to be useful must be complemented with a skill for suggesting relevant story ideas or content that you're promoting. If it's observed that a journalist for a technology publication likes infographics, create a blog post curating compelling graphics and then send that journalist a link to, or even mention his or her name in, the post as being the inspiration. When it's relevant, the journalist may mention the blog post and even link back to it. Editorial links that are also easy to share socially are the new currency for ranking content on the search and social web. The relationship can be mutually beneficial, too. Bloggers and journalists are always looking for stories or perspectives they can use, and you are looking for media coverage and the sharing of your content. It's a win for readers, too, when great stories are shared in relevant ways to interested communities.

The key to effective content promotion through social channels is to provide social networks, your community, and search engines with a steady stream of relevant, interesting content that gets shared and linked to. Those behaviors are powerful signals that will be rewarded with top search visibility and mentions wherever your prospects are looking.

## POWER UP WITH LINKS

Links are like electricity, and web pages are the lightbulbs of SEO. Google's PageRank is a representation of link authority for web pages and has been a key area of focus for most SEO professionals since Google came on the scene in the late 1990s. While the importance of links between websites for rankings is being debated by some in the SEO industry, the ability for links to deliver visitors to brand content and serve as a conduit to content for search engine bots remains essential.

The biggest asset for attracting links is content that is worth linking to. In the same way that you plan content for specific audiences in terms of motivating them to a particular outcome, certain kinds of content are prone to inspire people to link. As long as you expect to attract search and referral traffic to your content, you'll want to engage in ongoing link acquisition.

One of the most effective tactics for link building is to create content on other websites that links back to whatever page you're promoting. Bloggers and news websites are constantly on the lookout for contributors, so finding relevant websites that accept guest posts, or those that can be persuaded with your great content to accept a guest post, can become some of the most valuable links to acquire. Content creation is one of the highest-impact SEO tactics, but it's also one of the hardest.[2]

## USE CASE SCENARIOS FOR LINK-BUILDING STRATEGY

There are many different link-building tactics, but a proper link-building strategy must first consider the nature of the website being promoted and its starting point. To provide some context, here are three common starting points for link building that my team at TopRank Marketing has encountered numerous times over the past 10 years. Understanding your starting point can help guide you where you want to go.

### A Shiny, New, and Linkless Website

If a website is brand new and just launching, pay attention to the authority and relevance of the first sites that link to that resource. Many new companies would do well to consider publicity and media promotion as worthwhile investments for creating awareness for buyers as well as industry bloggers and media. Submitting a new domain name to 500 third-rate directories and social profiles, never to be used again, doesn't paint a very useful picture to Bing or Google compared with links from on-topic bloggers, local or trade media, and industry news websites.

With a new website, managing expectations is important, especially if the business is in a competitive category. The quality of links (i.e., sources that are authoritative and relevant) will always be more important than the quantity of links, but certainly the ideal is to achieve both. Linking strategy for new websites often focuses on social channels, as well as long-tail keyword phrases, for which the company can gain visibility more quickly.

### An Established and Randomly Linked Website

In contrast to a new website, a company site that has been around for 10 years and has engaged in media relations activities, advertising, and content creation may have a substantial number of links from a wide variety of credible sources. However, if the business has never invested in link building with specific attention to source, anchor text, and destination, then the impact may not be so beneficial. Without SEO insight, inbound links to the company may use random anchor text to mismatched destination pages, causing the presence but not the relevance that link building can achieve. As a result, the link sources may be diverse in a way that does not give a specific keyword-rich signal related to the topic that for which a web page or digital asset is most relevant. Linking to a home page 5,000 times using the anchor text "click here" is not nearly as meaningful as using "Tom's Natural Toothpaste" and linking to a web page specifically about natural toothpaste. You should try to reclaim links with requests to link sources to modify the code to use more desirable anchor text in order to make the links more useful to search engines and the people who click them.

### A Heavily but Questionably Linked Website

Our third starting point example is of a website that has a substantial number of links—an almost unbelievable number of links. This situation is one in which a company, or its gray-hat SEO agency, has acquired links using methods that are not in compliance with Google's recommended best practices. In other words, it may have been buying links from other websites for the specific purpose of increasing search engine rankings or, worse, resorting to old-school black-hat SEO tactics such as using bots to create links from the comments of blogs that haven't posted in more than six months. Such tactics may have worked in the past (or may even still work), but it is inevitable that either the search engine will identify the tricks or competitors will turn the company in to create an advantage for themselves. In many cases, these tactics can cause a website to be removed from search results altogether, causing serious damage to the business, since it cannot attract new customers through search. In cases of "spammy" links, they need to be identified and removed. At the same time, a qualitative link-building strategy based on useful, optimized content should be initiated to balance the percentage of good links with those that are not well regarded.

## LINK-BUILDING TACTICS

Now that we have some of the groundwork established with a few example approaches to link building, we can get into the tactics designed to provide a variety of quality links to optimized content.

### Link Audit

A link audit consists of identifying a baseline of your current inbound link footprint. It answers questions about the quantity, quality, source, and anchor text of the links to the website you are trying to promote. There are several tools to help you do this, including MajesticSEO.com and OpensiteExplorer.org. (See Figure 12.2.)

**FIGURE 12.2    Majestic SEO Backlinks**

Link research and tracking tools will give you a way to identify the current linking profile of your website, the linking profile of competitors, new link opportunities, trends in link acquisition over time, and the different types of links that are currently in place. Link types and attributes include:

- Anchor text links
- Follow or no-follow links
- Image links
- Redirected links
- Links from other web pages

Measuring information about the links to relevant pages of your website from other websites will help identify the quantity and quality of your website's link health compared to other sites that may be outperforming you on target keyword phrases. Considerations with a link audit include the following:

- What search-friendly links have you acquired over time?
- What is the authority and topical relevance of the link sources to your site?
- What pages do they link to?
- What anchor text is used with links to your site? Is it relevant to your destination pages?
- Which links are broken?
- Which areas of your site have too few links or irrelevant links?
- Where are the social link sources, and to what pages?
- What type of content attracts the most relevant links?

After auditing the link health of your own website and doing some competitive link research, you can go about developing your link-building approach.

### Develop a Link Strategy

The link-building strategy that is best for your website will be based on a variety of factors, including the content you have to promote, the keywords you are targeting, the competitiveness of your category, the amount and quality of new content you are going to publish and promote, your social network participation and size, internal resources, and expected rate of link acquisition. (See Figure 12.3.) Acquiring links individually or one by one can be very time-consuming, so a link strategy should account for finding the right mix of high-value targeted links as well as tactics that will scale link acquisition. Ultimately, the goal of link building is to drive direct traffic as well as provide search engines with a relevant quantity of signals to aid in crawling and ranking web pages.

Link strategies can vary according to these considerations. For example, a new website that has 50 web pages may decide to employ a mix of online PR tactics for its initial link building. Some of those tactics could include:

- Press releases sent through online news distribution services like PRWeb or PRNewswire
- Guest posts published on other blogs

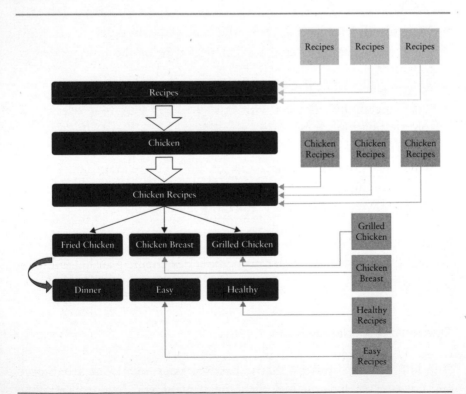

**FIGURE 12.3    Link-Building Grid**

- Contributed articles in industry publications
- Links from industry publications
- Rated lists of prominent, well-networked individuals or resources in the industry
- Infographics that represent compelling views or data relevant to the target market
- Contrarian views or counterpoints to trending news in the industry (with comments shut off on the blog, forcing others to link to you when responding from their own blogs)

Op-ed pieces can also be very valuable, because newspapers and similar publications are often viewed as an authoritative and credible source of content. Links from the online version of a news website can send traffic and substantial link popularity.

In the second example above, we discussed a site in which links exist, but are not focused. An effort may be made to update content that has the most links and to reach out to those link sources and ask if they will change the anchor text to use words more consistent with the optimization of the destination pages. A successful modification of anchor text could result in a notable number of on-target, on-topic inbound links to your website, giving Google and users a crystal clear idea of what the destination page is about. Link text such as "more information" is ambiguous and simply not helpful to readers or search engines in understanding the topic of the destination page.

For the site with abundant risky links, the strategy might start with the identification of unsavory links in the link portfolio and an effort to disengage from the purchase of those links. In the case of having "bad neighborhoods" linking to your website, requests can be sent to site owners to remove the links. Search engines understand that sites cannot control who links to them, so a focus on increasing the percentage or ratio of good links to those that are not is a better investment than chasing link removal from obscure scraper websites.

### How to Evaluate Links and Link Sources

Hunting individual links is rarely scalable, but some things are important to know when it comes to evaluating a good link. Examples of what makes a good link include:

- Overall domain authority
- Quantity and quality of inbound links to the source page
- How on-topic the source page is
- Whether the link includes the exact-match anchor text
- An annotation or descriptive text next to the link
- The number of other outbound links on the same page
- The age of the link
- Position of link on the page
- Whether the link is follow or no-follow
- Social shares of the link

A good link should deliver relevant visitors to your website and provide search engines with a clear and focused topical connection between the source and destination pages. Some important considerations for link evaluation include:

- *Link relevance*. If the link comes from a site that is relevant to your topic, it is worth much more than a link that is unrelated to your subject matter.
- *Link authority*. This is based on how authoritative the source of the link is. There are a couple types of authoritative sources. One example might be a site like that of the *New York Times*. Because the *New York Times* is a widely distributed media source, it is assumed that attention to detail is paid when it comes to fact checking. Another type of authoritative site might be an expert source on a niche topic, such as searchenginewatch.com. While these two types of sites are very different, they are similar in the fact that they are well respected and known for releasing quality information.
- *Link trust*. This relates to how trusted a link source is. If you have a large number of links coming from a source that is known for spamming, those links will not be of as much value as those from a trusted destination.

### Basic Link-Building Tactics

Once you have run an audit of your existing links and determined what makes a quality link, it's time to search for targeted link sources. The outreach, content, and social promotion discussed earlier in the chapter will achieve awareness, traffic, and links, but in most cases you have no control over the anchor text with links that come from promoted content. A combination of editorially diverse link sources and anchor text in conjunction with targeted and specific text used to link to your web pages is the winning combination for building link authority to your content.

As it relates to link building, content is the promise, and if the content is true to what customers care about, and the promotional language is relevant and executed properly, the links built as a result of that promise will be beneficial to your SEO strategy. Beyond promotion of great content, there can be a lot of value for basic link building with specifically targeted keyword phrases.

### Backlink Analysis

Competing search results with rankings higher than your pages often have certain sites linking to them that are not linking to your site. Backlink analysis is a tedious, but necessary, link research tactic to identify competitive link opportunities. The process can be pretty straightforward:

- When you are not logged into a search engine, do a search for one of your target keyword phrases.
- Document the URLs of pages and media that rank organically in the top 5 or 10 search results for your target keyword phrase.
- Import the URLs of those pages into a tool such as MajesticSEO.com to identify the quantity and quality of links to each of the pages that are ranking in the top 10.
- Review the link sources to identify which sites are linking to competing search results that are not linking to any page on your website.
- Review the source pages to identify possible link opportunities. If a competitor link source is a list, e-mail the webmaster to add your site to the list. If the link source is a how-to article for a resource (non-commercial) website, write a new and improved version of the article and offer it to the site owner with a link back to your site for author credit. If the competitor link comes from a blog post, offer to write a guest post for that blog that offers a more compelling set of tips or a countering opinion that includes a link back to your site within the post or from author attribution.

Backlink analysis can be sped up with specialty SEO tools or by using an SEO expert who has deep experience with this kind of link research.

Longtime link-building experts, like my friend Eric Ward, at http://letter
.ly/linkmosesprivate, offer practical how-to information on finding high-
quality, editorially relevant links that are good for attracting customers
as well as search engines.

### Social Profiles

Some social media platforms will allow you to add your company website address and create a followable link. Typically, forms have to be
filled out, and the intention of those sites is that you will actually participate. If you simply add a link and never take any action, then the link
that you acquired is not going to be worth much. A link source page is
only worth as much as the quantity of quality links pointing to it from
other websites.

### Commenting

Websites or blogs that allow comments can be excellent link sources
because you control the content around your link. Comments should
always be useful, and it's worth spending the extra time to provide helpful insights and then link to resources that you've published on your own
website or blog. Many blogs employ the rel=nofollow attribute to their
comment management systems, but those links can still send visitors, and
the content of the comments you make can inspire the authors to include
your link destination as a rel=follow link in their next blog post.

### Social Sharing and Bookmarks

Encourage social bookmarks and news submissions of your content via
services using passive methods like a widget embedded in the template
of your article pages or blog posts. Make it easy to share and save your
content to social destinations. Some social bookmarking services will
make a copy of what you bookmark or a static web page of the bookmarked content, including a crawlable link back to the source.

### Guest Posts

Write for blogs and include a link to your content in the body copy or in
your author bio. In the course of getting to know websites that already
rank well on the keyword phrases you're targeting, you may notice that
they often accept guest posts. Contact the website owners or blog editors
and suggest a compelling post that would be valuable to their readers.

If it makes sense editorially to link from within the guest post to your own website, be sure to use relevant keywords as the anchor text. Guest posts can be one of the highest-impact targeted link-building tactics you can use. The icing on the cake with guest posts is that the links are not only good signals for search engines but that high-profile sites can send substantial traffic as well.

### Curated Lists and Directories

Directories are not as effective as they once were, but there are specific directories for both blogs and websites that still serve useful purposes. At TopRank's Online Marketing Blog, we manage a list of more than 100 blog directory submission links at www.toprankblog.com/rss-blog-directories/. Don't expect a lot of traffic from these links, but niche links can augment an overall linking effort. If a quality directory has a relevant category with other reputable websites or blogs in it, then it may make sense for your content to be among them as a useful information source. Curated lists have been around as long as the web has. In fact, curated lists of links were pretty much how people discovered new content before search engines existed. Every industry has websites and blogs that collect and link to useful resources. Find those quality lists, and suggest your site or specially created on-topic content as another valid resource to be added.

### Job Listings

When promoting jobs for your company on the web, always include a link back to your site. Job postings are often syndicated to aggregators, so one listing may be promoted to multiple syndication partners as well as shared on social networks. We worked with an industry association that wanted to attract more traffic to its job listings pages. This national association had many regional chapters throughout the United States. In order to inspire relevant links back to the main job listing page, the headquarters offered the regional websites a widget to embed that would show new job listings automatically. The widget also included a clean, do-follow link back to the main job listings page on the national association website. As a result, the regional sites were able to provide a useful feature to their website at no cost, giving members reason to visit. The national association job listing pages received an increase in direct link traffic and a substantial increase in search engine traffic using keywords related to the link-building campaign.

### Contributed Articles

Industry websites and news and magazine websites often accept articles from subject matter experts. Establish a relationship by commenting on a news site, and share links to other content you've written for other credible websites and blogs. When you suggest a contributed article to the news or magazine site, consider these simple tips:

- The suggested article must be relevant to the publication and offer value to its readership. Original and thought-provoking ideas do well.
- Suggest ideas for more than one article. Share abstracts that include title and description, with a hook or premise for the article.
- Be prepared to show credible evidence of your work on your own site or other highly credible sites that you've contributed to.
- Don't be discouraged, but do be persistent. Don't suggest the same thing over and over. Tie your ideas into current news and trends in a way that offers insight that competitor publications are not covering.

### Press Releases

Many companies limit the publishing of press releases to their own website or through e-mail to a handful of industry journalists and bloggers. To potentially gain a substantial number of links from other relevant news sites and blogs, distribute press releases through a wire service. I have been using PRWeb since 2001 in this way (parent company Vocus is a TopRank client) and have received as few as 10 and as many as 1,500 inbound links (to a single press release) from different domain names as a result of distributing it through PRWeb. Really good releases might get 100 unique inbound links, but with today's common methods of discovering, consuming, and interacting with news, they'll also attract social shares. Many blogs and other news sites subscribe to new release distribution services like PRNewswire, Business Wire, Marketwire, and PRWeb. When those news sites and blogs see press releases they like, they will often republish the press release, including good links back to your website. Journalists use news search to look up past press releases and research stories, which presents another opportunity to be found and linked to.

### Sponsored Content

Many newsletters in different industries accept advertising or sponsorship. Newsletters sent via e-mail are often archived online or have landing pages that can be found through an index, through links from the company website, or through search. We discussed optimizing internal company newsletters for search in Chapter 10, which can drive additional traffic. Find newsletters in your industry that will link back to your website if you buy an ad or contribute a short article. The exposure through e-mail can drive traffic to your website, and the online version of the newsletter that includes your ad or guest article with link can help send even more traffic and assist with search engine ranking. This is a situation whereby a newsletter that accepts guest articles or ads also happens to archive past issues online in a way that can be found by search engines. Purchasing links outright for SEO purposes is against Google's terms of use.

### Reviewing Blogs and Offering a Badge

My company's BIGLIST of search marketing blogs has resulted in over 64,000 inbound links to our company blog from relevant search marketing blogs, many of which are competitors to our agency. (See Figure 12.4.) When reviewing blogs, be sure to focus on quality, and be consistent. Offer reviewed blogs a way to show off their recognition in the form of a widget or badge that links back to the list or recognition page. Include your blog's logo on the badge for improved brand awareness whether blogs use it to link back to your site or not.

### Live Blogging

If you attend an industry conference, live blogging presentations can be a great tactic for building links. Sometimes, the presenters mentioned in the posts will link to the live blog post as media coverage for their company. Still others will link and share on the social web because there is no other record of their presentation.

**FIGURE 12.4   TopRank BIGLIST Blogs**

## SOCIAL LINKS

Social links are basically the links included in status updates, tweets, and links included from other social sharing platforms. For the most part, links that come from social media websites employ a no-follow attribute that instructs search engine crawlers not to follow those links for discovery or ranking purposes. But there are some instances where those links do count, according to an interview with Danny Sullivan conducted by representatives from Bing and Google, and there has been confirmation from both major algorithmic search engines that they do consider links within social media content to determine ranking.[3]

While Google uses more than 200 different signals, including PageRank, to determine how pages are ranked, links discovered in public social streams can also have influence on web page rankings. With Google's Search plus Your World update in January 2012, the importance of social content sharing and growing your social network is just as important, or more so, than old-fashioned links. The volume and quality of social interaction, coupled with the influence of those you're interacting with, can have a noticeable impact on the search visibility of your content for people logged in to Google.

## KEYWORD TO LINK MAPPING FOR SUCCESS

When planning your link-building strategy, map your list of keyword targets to the types of optimized content you'll be promoting. The focal point of your content-based link-building tactics should be concentrated on search phrases or social topics your brand wants to be known for and found under. At the same time, it's okay to use some variations of those keywords. Not every website will link to your web page exactly the same way. In fact, it would probably look unnatural if your website had 5,000 new links from different domain names in one week all using the exact same anchor text. Focus on content your customers care about, and optimize that content for search phrases, social topics, and especially for social shares and inbound links. Make it drop-dead easy for search engines to see your content as the authority on topics that matter to your customers. With a quantity of quality links that are relevant, your content will light up on the search and social web, bringing more customers and attracting even more links.

## ACTION ITEMS

1. Identify your top social networks for content promotion relevant to your audience.
2. Research influential members of those communities, bloggers, and journalists.
3. Determine what types of content attract a quantity of quality social shares and links within your topics and networks.
4. Research the link profile of your own website and competitor websites to identify where they are getting links and you are not.
5. Research blogs and industry publications to find those that accept guest posts, contributed articles, or places where your own content can be syndicated.

# CHAPTER 13

## Progress, Refinement, and Success: Measurement

Armed with goals and a plan, the fruit of our integrated search and social media content marketing efforts must be determined through proper measurement. There are many dimensions to assessing an optimized and socialized content marketing program, enough to fill several more books. A good foundation for success will be to emphasize the role of measurement according to the influence of content across the buying and customer life cycle. From awareness to advocacy, content plays an important role and through an adaptive process of hypothesis, benchmarking, assessment, and refinement, businesses can create competitive advantages and value for their relationships with customers.

Whether you're trying to attract more customers through search engines or social networks, the relationship between setting goals and measuring performance must be in close alignment for a successful effort to reach overall marketing and business goals. Organizations have many reasons for publishing digital content, and while our attention to goals has focused on marketing and sales objectives, it also extends to other communications, audiences, and business benefits. In Chapter 4 we discussed setting goals for increasing leads and sales as well as to improve media coverage, attract talented employees, and serve online customers more efficiently. In this chapter I will explore some of the key considerations for measuring content marketing performance relevant to the overall goals of attracting and engaging more customers with particular emphasis on key performance indicators and objectives associated with optimizing content and social media engagement.

## APPROACH TO INTEGRATED CONTENT MARKETING MEASUREMENT

All measurement must have a starting point, and an important part of establishing a baseline of integrated search and social media marketing performance is to identify goals. Broader business goals related to content marketing often go beyond an "increase in sales" to include:

- Elevate brand perception
- Establish thought leadership
- Drive customer engagement
- Provide better customer service
- Increase customer retention
- Grow customer advocacy and referrals

Content plays an essential role in helping organizations achieve a range of business goals and the intentional optimization and social promotion of that content can improve the speed and relevance of how a brand connects with both prospects and existing customers.

## THE ROLE OF SEARCH ENGINE OPTIMIZATION KEY PERFORMANCE INDICATORS (KPIs)

Earlier, I mentioned the adage that "facts tell and stories sell," so to help you understand the role of analytics and measurement within a search engine optimized content marketing plan, I'll use a story set in the context of a Minnesota winter.

If there is too little snow, Jason, Eric, and Bill will not be able to go on their snowmobile trip. To ensure their plans aren't foiled, each sets out to measure the amount of flakes on the ground.

Jason meticulously counts each individual snowflake. While incredibly accurate, his process stretches across such a long period that by the time it's complete, he forgets exactly what he is measuring and what he should be doing with the data he is gathering.

Eric takes one look outside and determines that the amount of snow is "not enough." He retreats inside, thinking his potential trip a failure.

Bill, meanwhile, develops formulas designed to measure exactly how many inches of snow are on the ground, and more specifically, how many inches have fallen on the portions of land that will make up his snowmobile route.

Days later, it turns out that Jason's individual counting method was the most accurate form of measurement. And Eric was absolutely right in the sense that there just "wasn't enough" snow on the ground. But despite being less accurate than Jason and less vast in scope than Eric, Bill was the only one that day who enjoyed a successful snowmobile trip. He did not allow himself to get hung up in minutiae—yet he refused to accept an overly big-picture view.

How does this analogy apply to measurement of optimized content marketing metrics? Let's start with two basic truths: (1) Absolutely everything can be measured, and (2) the big picture can be misleading (especially if you are aiming toward very specific objectives, as discussed in Chapter 4).

Let's explore the danger of minutiae. Logging in to your web analytics reporting platform such as Google Analytics will provide you with nearly every possible metric you've ever cared to measure about a website or blog. Are you interested in how many visitors landed on your home page by typing the keyword "red widgets" into Google and who stayed longer than five minutes? You'll find the answer in minutes. Need to segment this red widget information further to measure the amount of traffic that came from Facebook in Singapore? Just a few seconds more. When evaluating website metrics, there is no difficulty in finding the data you want to measure—just as the ridiculously tedious act of counting snowflakes is extraordinarily simple. The level of difficulty increases when deciding *what* to measure rather than determining *how* to measure.

So, what do we need to measure? The most basic, highest-level KPI that should be measured for a search-focused content marketing campaign is the traffic generated by organic search. Is this metric increasing or decreasing in line with your efforts? Organic search traffic is one metric that anyone responsible for an online marketing budget will be most interested in seeing improve—and so it is a metric that holds a great deal of importance.

While Google has implemented encrypted search for logged-in users of Google services, all is not lost with the ever-increasing frequency of referring search phrases labeled "not provided." Within the SEO community there has been no shortage of speculation about how to infer meaning from the masked Google search phrases, from extrapolation based on historical search phrase data associated with specific pages to pulling in data from Google Webmaster tools. Near the time of its announcement, Google forecast the percentage of "not provided" traffic at less than double digits, but along with many of my SEO industry peers, I've seen our own percentage of masked keyword traffic approach 26 percent. With the growing popularity of Google+, there is no reason to think that number will do anything but increase.

Most analytics and optimization experts are still adjusting to encrypted search causing referring keyword phrases to be designated "not found" but there are a few things content marketers can do to interpret and find meaning. The 75 to 90 percent of organic keyword traffic that is not encrypted can be used as a sort of proxy for understanding the distribution of referring keywords that are encrypted. Also, when keywords are mapped to specific pages and the organic search traffic is increasing or decreasing to those pages over time, associations with keyword ranking provided by Google Webmaster Tools and other 3rd party ranking tools can help provide content marketers with some insight as to keyword performance. These tactics and many more can be helpful at filling the void of "not provided," but the direct correlation of specific referring organic keywords to conversions for the 5 to 25 percent of encrypted search queries performed on Google is gone.

## THE VALUE OF SEO FOR CONTENT MARKETING

Measuring the return on investment of optimized content on marketing and business goals relies on a number of factors including: The ongoing investment made by the brand in SEO activities, the effect of search traffic on PR, customer service and job listing content, the advertising equivalent of organic search visibility and traffic, the value of conversions from organic search, order size, order frequency and even the cost of not implementing SEO. Determining the value of implementing SEO best practices should factor the body of content a brand publishes over time, not just a single landing page over a few months. The impact of publishing optimized and well-linked web pages is cumulative over time. The more optimized pages that are published, the more possible entry points there are to brand content through search, links from other websites and social shares.

For SEO programs that have been able to achieve some momentum, individual conversion rates can be calculated for groups of keywords, individual keywords, for categories of content and for individual landing pages. Attribution models can be tricky, so keep in mind the overall consumer journey and sales cycle when determining the conversion value of SEO on specific pieces of content. Relying solely on the last click rarely tells the entire conversion story.

Other important search engine optimization KPIs include: keyword phrase position in search results, aggregate social shares such as Google+ votes per web page, inbound links from third-party websites to each web page, visitors from organic search (brand and non-branded phrases), visitors from links, and visitors from social media sites managed by the brand.

As a common marketing tactic, SEO is often held accountable for attracting visitors that are actively looking for answers, into a conversion of some kind. Those conversions might be a transaction like a purchase from an online store or an indication of interest such as downloading a report, signing up for a webinar, registering for a newsletter, demo or free trial. Using our holistic content marketing perspective, those conversions might also be a journalist inquiry on the newsroom, a candidate application for an open position, or the five-star rating of an FAQs page.

Beyond websites, SEO can attract search traffic to blogs and brand social media content on and off the corporate website. Social media optimization goals for improving social network growth and engagement because of discovery through search should be included in the KPIs and SEO program performance metrics right along with broader traffic and conversion goals.

There is often an inherent problem with focusing on one large overall metric: A lack of context. For instance, say your organic search traffic has decreased 15 percent over the past two months. It may be very tempting to view the current amount of organic traffic as "not enough" and paint your SEO and content marketing efforts as a failure. But a slightly deeper look reveals that, although total organic search has decreased, organic search traffic generated by keywords that you have focused on during optimization and content marketing efforts (i.e., "red widgets") has increased. Better yet, visitors who arrive at your site with variations of these keywords are converting (i.e., completing an action ranging from submitting a form to finalizing a sale). In this case, with some very basic context pulled from the most basic analytics reports, we can determine that the portions of our campaigns that we have most recently optimized for are proving to be successful. We can also put into place a plan to replicate this success, either by creating more content optimized for red widgets or by applying the same principles to a new category.

The role of SEO with measures of success isn't just about converting keyword queries into sales, although that's certainly important. SEO can improve the search visibility of any kind of content—from news to job listings to customer support. Set goals and develop a hypothesis about what the impact of increased search visibility could do for improving the performance of your content for customers that are actively in a search for answers. Identify the key performance metrics that are indications toward success for content types, personas, and across the buying and customer lifecycle. Take benchmark measurements for those key metrics as well as for overall program success measurements. Analyze performance on an ongoing basis and make improvements to scale what's working and reoptimize what isn't.

## SOCIAL MEDIA KEY PERFORMANCE INDICATORS (KPIS)

The question regarding whether social media's true impact on online marketing efforts can be measured is one that has been asked countless times—with strong cases on both sides of the fence. Ultimately, the important question is whether social media can be directly measured. At the most basic level, you can see this by simply logging in to your web analytics account and looking at the referring traffic report. If you see social networks as referring sources such as Facebook, Twitter, or LinkedIn, you know which social media sites are driving traffic to your website.

Of course, this direct measurement, while worth tracking, goes somewhat against the idea of what social media is about. Social media helps build connections. Connections, in turn, can help to build inquiries and sales. To attempt to draw a direct line from one to the other, while possible, is akin to drawing a direct connection between a snowy day and a snowmobile trip. The snowy day makes the conditions right for a snowmobile trip, but it doesn't directly cause a trip to be taken—unless you've already previously established this connection in your mind.

That said, if direct measurement of social media is nebulous, what should we be looking at to determine its success?

One quantifiable KPI is the total number of connections with brand social properties or individuals that represent the brand, which could mean those who "like" your company on Facebook or those who are following your updates on Twitter. It certainly applies to the number of people who have added your brand's Google+ page to their circles. When your brand is included in others' Google+ circles, the likelihood of your content appearing in their search results while logged in is substantially greater. The number of examples for social engagement being correlated to an impact on sales has increased significantly over the past year. For example, over 50 percent of Twitter followers are more likely to purchase from brands they follow.[1]

Likewise, a corresponding article in *USA Today* indicates that Coca-Cola Facebook fans are 10 times more likely to purchase than nonfans.[2] As noted previously, this is not a direct line from "Facebook" to "sale," but rather an indication that building connections in social media can be measured, in part, by a correlating increases in bottom line objectives.

Another quantifiable metric that can contribute to both bottom-line objectives and to building more effective social connections is the amount of shares, comments, links, or citations. All of these actions can be found within traditional search results. Think of these metrics the same way you would think of conversation at a business dinner party. If your guests are sharing what you say with others, making commentary on your statements, linking conversation to a statement you had previously made, or even citing past statements you made, you would have a very vibrant and dynamic conversation. Would this conversation immediately lead to these customers purchasing your goods or signing a contract? Probably not. But depending on that potential client or customer's need—and the vibes they feel after the party commences—it is by no means out of line to suggest that these conversations could directly and positively impact your bottom line the next day, week, month, or year.

Put simply, we buy from those we feel a stronger, more personal connection with. Social media may digitize this, but it's Relationship Building 101. And the strength of your relationships is not always something you directly measure, but rather something you attribute to your bottom-line success.

## KEY SOCIAL MEDIA METRICS

Social media is a fantastic platform for content discovery, sharing, engagement and influence both short and long term. Consumer behaviors in a social media and networking context can be very different from the explicit intentions common with search. And yet, consumers do tap into their social networks for specific recommendations that lead to purchase. Brands are indeed creating incentives and offers for product and services that consumers act on. Social commerce is a reality and that makes social media metrics even more important.

I mentioned above the task of developing a hypothesis, which is an important question to answer with social media measurement. For example, let's say a simple hypothesis with a product blog and its effect on a sales objective goes like this:

> We think an increase in blog subscribers, comments, and social shares over the next six months will correlate with an 20 percent increase in inquiries and sales.

With that hypothesis, the brand can identify overall goals as well as individual KPIs. The insight into customer personas and what they care about is translated into an editorial calendar and efforts to optimize, attract links and engage on the social web. The performance of blog content and social engagement activities are monitored for their effect on goals and KPIs will indicate progress.

What actually gets measured depends on goals, but consider these key areas for social media focused content marketing: Revenue, Engagement, and Cost Savings.

### Revenue Goals:

- Speed of sales cycle
- Percent of repeat business
- Percent of customer retention
- Transaction value
- Referrals
- Net new leads
- Cost per lead
- Conversions from the community

**Engagement Goals:**

- Members
- Posts or threads
- Comments
- Inbound links
- Tags, votes, bookmarks, shares
- Referrals
- Post frequency

**Cost Savings Goals:**

- Issue resolution time
- Account turnover
- Employee turnover
- Hiring and recruiting
- Percent of issues resolved online

## BUSINESS OUTCOMES

Measuring business outcomes is about taking raw data and giving it context to the greatest degree possible. It is the difference between driving total traffic and driving quality traffic. It is the difference between total sales and sales of a product we are actively marketing.

Any conversation on business outcomes must start with a clear understanding of business objectives. As noted earlier in this chapter, measurement of your online marketing program can be both extremely broad and extremely granular. You can measure success based on both total traffic and individual visits from Facebook. And while both metrics have value, both also lack context, which is vital for your objectives. And without context, we can make decisions that are misguided—or we can become paralyzed from making any decision at all.

Let's circle back to three examples of very specific business goals shared in Chapter 4:

- Online public relations
- Human resources and recruiting
- Customer service objectives

In each scenario, broad metrics such as total traffic could help to indicate the success of these initiatives. In the same sense, individual visits from Facebook could also help to indicate the success of these initiatives. But would they really give us a clear picture that we could use to make actionable improvements?

Let's look at our online public relations example first. More so than any other objective on this list, this is the one that is most likely going to impact broader objectives, such as driving total traffic. The reason for this is that the goal of most public relations–related campaigns, with the exception of ultratargeted initiatives, is to reach a broader audience.

At their heart, public relations objectives are about boosting awareness for your brand. In regard to business outcomes, these can most directly be measured by major news channels or PR sites picking up your press releases and by media mentions of your brand. In a less direct sense, the value of online public relations can be measured by direct traffic to your site (or by users arriving at your website by typing your URL directly into a browser or accessing your site via a bookmark, which is a common report in any Google Analytics package).

Online public relations measurement can go one step further, however, with the simple inclusion of SEO best practices. Say, for example, you introduce a new product into the market: red turbo widgets. You distribute a press release optimized for this phrase that links back to your website. Sometime later (e.g., a day, a week, or a month), you analyze your web results and see that the press release you distributed is appearing as a top referring source back to your website. This is a direct form of measurement indicating the success of this release. And, in looking at your keyword report, you see that variations of "red turbo widgets" have increased steadily since distribution of your release. This is one step beyond pure measurement and into the realm of actionable data. In other words, there is strong evidence to suggest that your audience is interested in this new product—and you may attract more prospects by developing more types of content.

Other types of business outcomes, while perhaps less direct and bottom-line oriented, can be equally measured and shaped in a way that supports action.

Taking the second bulleted item, measuring your human resources and recruiting objectives, requires looking at the segment of results you are most trying to influence and, potentially, the portion of your website you are most striving to drive traffic to.

It's reasonable to suggest that if you were to develop a job listing for an SEO copywriter, you would host this information somewhere on your site. If so (and this is the beautiful thing), you would be well on the way to being able to measure the results of literally any source, ranging from search to social, that could help contribute to the success of this listing.

For instance, properly segmenting your landing page report in your analytics platform (i.e., a report indicating where on your site visitors landed) can provide you with details regarding not only how many people visited your job listing page over a specified period of time, but also which keywords they used to find this page. This data can provide you the information you need to reoptimize or test new messaging on this page in order to drive even more search traffic.

Furthermore, segmenting this report to show referring sources rather than just referring keywords can provide a clear indication of which social sources are actually driving the most interest. For instance, did your page receive 45 visits from LinkedIn but only 10 from Facebook? This may be an indication that your recruitment efforts for the position in question, from a social perspective, are best served by LinkedIn, and more of your effort should center on this platform.

The king of all measurement factors in regard to human resources is quality job applicants. Setting up your online job listing as an online job application—and setting up an appropriate form-completion goal in your analytics platform—can tell you how many applicants your page converted and which keyword or source drove these applicants. To circle back to our social example, let's say that you received five applicants from LinkedIn (out of 45 visits), only two of which were quality. On the other hand, you received five applicants (out of 10 visits) from Facebook, four of which were quality. You now have a quantifiable measurement indicating that Facebook, in fact, may just be the stronger recruiting platform for your needs. With this data in hand, you can choose to spend more time either recruiting on Facebook or building up your candidate network in LinkedIn.

Finally, in our last example of customer support, it may be that you do not need to measure success by any traditional factor such as online traffic or inquiries. Instead, you might be more focused on how users are interacting with your site.

To revisit our example from Chapter 4, pretend you are a manufacturer of universal remotes and you have discovered that each call to your customer service line costs you $32.50. To decrease costs, you develop a new FAQs page designed to answer some of the most common questions your call center receives. Using the landing pages report in your web analytics platform, you can identify how many visits this page is capturing each month. You can even correlate this information to a second graph, pulled from your call center's log reports, showing the total volume of calls day by day. If this report is trending downward at the same time your new FAQs page traffic is trending upward, you have strong data to suggest that this new page is earning its keep on your website.

And because you can always take things one step further to make actionable decisions, you may also determine that, based on the types of keywords that are driving traffic to this page, there exists a much broader range of questions in the minds of your users. This can help you justify the decision to add content to your FAQs page, as needed, or even to create a second page to address a new set of questions.

Additionally, while looking at the types of calls your call center continues to receive, you may determine that most customer support calls focus on a handful of specific features. This can provide the data you need to update pages on your website that are related to these features (through the addition of hyperlinks or calls to action) so you can more effectively funnel visitors to FAQs pages, and this helps you save money by reducing customer support calls.

## ANALYTICS TOOLS

Perhaps the most fundamental measurement question you may ask (apart from, "What should we be measuring?") is, "How should we be measuring it?"

In regard to search and social media measurement and analytics tools, there are a number of applications and services available. Unfortunately, there is no "one size fits all" solution, but with the right understanding of KPIs, overall goals, and process for evaluation and improvement, you'll be able to narrow down your choices. Many individual social platforms offer their own analytics, such as LinkedIn business pages statistics, YouTube Insight, or Facebook Insights, as complementary services or bundled with advertising services. There are also several third-party web analytics and social media measurement tools to consider:

## Web Analytics:

- Google Analytics is the most full featured free analytics tool and has a social tracking plugin.
- Clicky is a real-time, low-cost web analytics tool.
- HubSpot offers inbound marketing software including web analytics.
- Adobe SiteCatalyst is an advanced feature, real-time analytics solution.
- KISSmetrics offers customer analytics for improving conversions and retention.

## SEO Measurement:

- Advanced Web Ranking is a suite of tools including search result rank tracking.
- SEOmoz PRO and Raven Tools both offer rank checking options and basic social monitoring.
- Majestic SEO is a premium link-tracking tool.
- SEMRush identifies organic keyword visibility tracking for Google on any website.
- Google Webmaster Tools provides detailed reports about web page visibility on Google.
- Bing Webmaster Tools provides data on search queries, crawling, and search traffic for websites on Bing.
- BrightEdge is a premium social media SEO performance metrics and reporting tool.
- Conductor offers a suite of enterprise SEO tools and performance reporting options.

## Social Media Monitoring:

- Trackur offers low to mid-range pricing options for social media monitoring.
- Sprout Social offers a low-cost social media monitoring and management solution.
- Alterian SM2 is a full featured social media monitoring toolset.

- Vocus Social Media Software offers a social media monitoring solution includes sentiment and influencer tracking (TopRank client).
- Radian6 is a premium social media monitoring and crm solution.

**Social Media Analysis Tools:**

- PeopleBrowsr offers social media analytics and competitor analytics.
- EdgeRank Checker offers analysis for Facebook news feed optimization.
- AddThis sharing widget offers sharing analytics.
- Bit.ly url shortening also offers basic analytics on shared URLs.

There are many other web analytics tools to provide insight into the KPIs that will provide indications toward the progress you desire. Keeping business and marketing goals in mind related to website marketing performance, tool identification, testing, implementation, and scale is a much more efficient process.

There are volumes more to be said about search and social media analytics, but these insights about measuring content marketing performance will definitely get you started. They are a framework to help you understand the business goals and measurement relationship as well as the importance of developing a perspective toward measurement hypothesis, benchmarking, assessment and refinement. Now go forth, market, and measure!

**ACTION ITEMS**

1. Identify your overall business goals and those related specifically to marketing, customer service, public relations, and recruiting.
2. Identify specific content-related objectives for each content type above. What are the SEO and social media KPIs for each?
3. What hypothesis do you have about how SEO will help you reach a particular content marketing goal? How?
4. Identify KPIs for that goal, take benchmark measurements, and implement social media and SEO tactics with corresponding content.
5. Using social media monitoring and web analytics tools, assess content performance, and reoptimize or scale accordingly.

# PHASE 3

# SCALE

# CHAPTER 14

## Optimize and Socialize: Processes and Training

With a solid content marketing strategy and tactical mix in place, it's time to think about how to integrate an "optimize and socialize" approach into your overall online marketing program. Many companies start content-focused SEO and social media marketing efforts within specific departments like marketing or public relations. For larger organizations, a particular business unit or division might serve as a test case. Regardless of where you start, once those initial efforts are under way, the next step is to gain broader adoption and momentum by understanding how to incorporate social media marketing and SEO best practices with your company's overall online content-creation efforts.

When supporting your company's resources for implementing a scalable "optimize and socialize" content marketing approach, consider the following: (1) where SEO and social media optimization fit within the content planning and publishing process and (2) the social media and SEO skills of content creators.

We've identified a number of processes and best practices in both phase 1 (planning) and phase 2 (implementation) of optimization. In this chapter, I will expand on several of those processes as they might apply to a few different situations. I also explore implications for training:

1. Small business with limited marketing resources
2. Midsized business with a small marketing/PR department
3. Enterprise with a corporate headquarters entity and multiple business units

## SMALL BUSINESS: NO TIME FOR CONTENT

Tom started his own video game accessories business five years ago and has enjoyed steady, yet modest, growth despite a fluctuating economic environment. Tom is a very hands-on boss with his small business and is doing most of the marketing himself, through his website, which attracts about 75 percent of the orders. He also manages an e-mail list and does some pay-per-click (PPC) advertising, which contributes to the remaining new business. Tom has tried starting and maintaining a presence on Facebook, Twitter, and several industry forums, but his time available for social networking has been reduced considerably. As a former corporate marketer, Tom realizes the importance of content for his website as well as a social presence. However, he simply doesn't have the time or resources . . . or so he thinks.

### Recommendations for Tom's Video Game Accessories Business

If Tom plans to continue to perform the marketing tasks for his small business himself, he'll want to be more intentional about how he uses his website to reach ideal customer segments instead of simply maintaining the site with content about products and services. Paying an outside resource to conduct an audit of his website and online marketing efforts may be a consideration. With a road map in place that identifies goals, key customer segments, and what motivates them to engage and buy, Tom can prioritize his time to work efficiently with the highest impact.

For the sake of this example, let's say Tom has determined to focus his efforts on content that answers key questions his ideal customers ask during the consideration and decision portions of the buying cycle. Knowing that it would be very difficult to achieve industry authority for generic search terms and social topics, Tom decides to capture prospective customers with content that answers important prerequisite questions before purchase. Tom's online marketing audit has identified search keywords and social topics as well as the content types and formats that will best attract, engage, and inspire his ideal prospective customers. With a more intentional plan in place, he understands what types of content he'll need to create and the channels where that content should be visible in order to attract the right customers.

### Training

Tom will need to consider his current skills and what he'll need to know in order to make better choices in regard to content planning, optimization, social promotion, and measurement. For example, if the audit indicates customers will be motivated by video content, then he'll want to brush up on his video editing skills or find a reasonable vendor he can outsource to. If Tom has other employees that have product expertise, he'll want to offer some kind of training in order for them to help with SEO copywriting, social network development, and engaging with customers on industry forums and social networks. One of the most important online marketing training investments Tom could make is with social media monitoring and web analytics. Google offers free online classes with Google Analytics that can be a great way to build a foundation for understanding how people find and engage with content on his website. A simple social media–monitoring tool like Trackur could give Tom a quick heads-up whenever the gaming community mentions his products or talks about his company.

### Process

An editorial plan that is thoughtful about customer needs and pain points will be instrumental for Tom's content-creation effectiveness, in both the short and long term. He can identify what content will be created and by whom, and he can determine the particular media formats to use. Content repurposing can be planned out with his customer e-mail newsletter and any other social or editorial promotion he's involved with. Along with planned content creation, optimization, and social promotion processes, Tom can schedule time between himself and several members of his staff for community engagement and social network development.

Following a schedule and set of processes will help Tom implement search- and social media–friendly content that best attracts, engages, and inspires his ideal prospects when they are looking to buy. Growing

> ### Three Key Phases of a Social, SEO, and Content Marketing Audit
>
> 1. **Discovery:** Research and document the current situation, goals, challenges, competitive environment, and resources.
> 2. **Assessment:** Review the current approach, process, SEO, and social media readiness. Evaluate current content marketing efforts and identify areas of opportunity.
> 3. **Recommendation:** Provide best practices social, SEO, and content marketing processes and tools.

his skills at content creation as well as monitoring and measurement will help Tom better evaluate the performance of his content marketing efforts and make adjustments accordingly. The longer Tom follows his plan and processes for content creation, optimization, and social network growth, the more entry points he'll create for customers to find out about his business through search engines, links, and social media referrals. Following a plan, improving skills, and enlisting help will provide Tom's business with improved search and social media visibility without taking too much time away from other responsibilities.

## MIDSIZED BUSINESS: SOCIAL COMMITMENT ISSUES

Melosa Software has hired search engine optimization (SEO) consultants for audits on its website in the past and has taken much of the SEO work in-house for handling by its IT and marketing departments. Content optimization efforts involve using keywords identified by a past SEO consultant in new content and with link-building efforts. SEO performance is measured with monthly keyword ranking reports and by monitoring keyword referrals to the company website using Google Analytics.

Internal employees in charge of both marketing and public relations initiatives are responsible for the creation of any new web pages, writing blog posts, and managing a handful of social media accounts, including Twitter, YouTube, and Facebook. Blogging consistently has been a challenge, and there simply hasn't been enough time to determine whether adding new social networks like Google+ makes sense. Turnover has caused gaps in continuity with blogging and social media involvement. The IT department provides basic monthly web analytics reports, and there is no social media reporting. There's speculation among the management team that blogging and social media participation aren't worth it if they can't measure the return on investment and if they can't keep up with blog posts. Management is also concerned that if social engagement and blogging are not consistent, the company will look out of date and inattentive to its customers. It's a classic case of, "If we don't try, no one will see us fail."

## Recommendations for Midsized Melosa Software

As with many midmarket companies, marketing and PR staff wear many hats at Melosa Software, and, while there have been previous efforts to develop a meaningful approach to attracting customers through search, the fast pace of change in the search marketing industry has exceeded the internal IT and marketing staff's ability to keep up. Information that was valid two years ago related to SEO or current social networking platforms and best practices is unlikely to be as valuable today, especially with significant changes that have occurred with Google, Facebook, and Twitter.

Melosa Software will benefit greatly from an update to its online marketing mix in terms of an evaluation of current marketing efforts and updates to its target customer profiles to account for consumer and technology changes in the search and social media landscape. With multiple departments creating content for the website, an overall content strategy would help identify target audiences for departmental content and define content topics, expected outcomes, and how multidepartmental content can work together. An assessment of search demand on important keywords as well as the nature of conversations within social networks on relevant topics will help Melosa Software identify where SEO and social media content will fit in the marketing mix. A social media, content, and SEO plan that identifies key topics, customer information needs for purchase and referral, appropriate social channels, and key performance indicators (KPIs) will help mitigate "social media failure" concerns, especially with solid social monitoring and web analytics in place to measure content, search, and social media performance.

### Training

With an updated content marketing, SEO, and social media plan, Melosa Software's marketing and PR staff can identify appropriate, high-impact tasks to manage, as well as which tasks can be performed by other staff and, potentially, outside resources. Many companies find they already have employees acting on behalf of the brand through their Facebook, Twitter, and Google+ accounts. Initiating an internal program to identify social media–savvy staff can reveal a useful internal network of resources. Direction, training, and support can be made available to those interested and qualified employees, and social media guidelines can be provided for all staff.

Marketing and PR can serve in an editorial capacity with internal subject matter experts in each product group contributing to blogging and SEO copywriting efforts. A coordinated content strategy will involve a content plan for departments across the company, including marketing, public relations, corporate, human resources and recruiting, customer service, and sales. Fundamental SEO copywriting training and social networking can be provided for content creators in each department, along with tools for measurement and feedback so they can see the impact their contributions are having at the departmental level and to the business overall.

Information technology staff can be provided with up-to-date technical SEO, social integration, and web analytics training in order to better support the rest of the organization. Tapping an outside consultant for a content marketing strategy review and recommendations quarterly or annually can give Melosa Software up-to-date insight into best practices while enabling the vast majority of implementation to be handled in-house.

### Process

A breakdown of responsibilities should be outlined in the content marketing, SEO, and social media plan, allowing better coordination among content producers across the Melosa Software organization. Workflow

## Components of a Social SEO and Content Marketing Audit

- Integrated social media, SEO, and content marketing strategy
- Social and SEO on- and off-site best practices and tactics
- Content promotion and link building
- Social network development
- Social media policy
- Recommended social, SEO, and content tools
- Implementation overview
- Approach to social media monitoring
- Program performance measurement: KPIs and business outcomes
- Benchmark measurements
- Ongoing implementation and program refinement guidelines

processes for content creation, optimization, social promotion, and measurement for each department will enable best-practices "optimize and socialize" content to scale. Search and social media management software may be a consideration to help provide centralized management portals for social content and asset optimization, promotion, and monitoring. The marketing and public relations group can provide content governance over all departments with input from editorial leaders within each function. A breakdown of the content production and marketing process will identify the role for each participant in terms of ensuring messaging, keyword optimization, content segmentation for relevant social channels, and where content will be repurposed.

By evaluating its current online and content marketing approach, Melosa Software can develop a customer-centric content marketing plan that integrates with search and social media best practices. Clearly defined goals, responsibilities, workflow, and reporting will enable interdepartmental cooperation that makes implementing relevant, consistent, and impactful content for search engine visibility and social media engagement an integral part of the marketing program.

## ENTERPRISE: TOO BIG NOT TO BE SOCIAL

With a corporate headquarters in the Midwest and more than 20 business units operating across the United States, Western Europe, and the Asia Pacific region, Giant Manufacturing has implemented various search, social, and content marketing initiatives across its various businesses with varying degrees of success. Regional marketing leaders take strategic direction from headquarters, but have the flexibility to customize content as appropriate by region and to run search and social media efforts considering regional preferences. Headquarters and five of the largest US operations, along with businesses in the United Kingdom and Hong Kong, have developed content plans and an effective social media presence through corporate blogs and on relevant regional networks. However, few have consistently implemented best-practices search and social media optimization, and only three of the businesses have achieved an effective level of integration between content, SEO, and social media marketing efforts.

In contrast with strategic best practices, a lack of global implementation of web and social media content has resulted in inconsistent buyer experiences across regional websites, less-than-ideal search and social media traffic, poor social network growth, and underprojected performance in online customer inquiries.

### Recommendations for Giant Manufacturing

When it comes to content, managing editorial initiatives across an enterprise that extends globally can be a challenge. Best practices for one region do not necessarily translate into best practices for all. There are many considerations for situations as expansive as international manufacturers from the need for a consistent global narrative to the importance of regional customization, but I'll focus on a few key points.

Giant Manufacturing has an opportunity to leverage a global content plan, social media strategy, and SEO best practices in order to bring consistent core messaging to its overall web properties. As with the small- and medium-sized business situations described earlier in this chapter, Giant Manufacturing could benefit from an online marketing audit to bring insight into overall core messaging relevant to customer segments, content plans, social media operations, and SEO guidelines. At the regional level, content marketing plans, social networking, and SEO functions can be coordinated accordingly. A portal that connects the different businesses' marketing staff with a library of content, media, and training materials updated by headquarters can bring a measure of governance and consistency across global content marketing.

### Training

To bring individual marketers in each business up to speed with best-practices content optimization and social promotion, an assessment could be developed to identify learning opportunities among content producers. Outside experts and internal search, social media, and content marketing champions could be enlisted to conduct webinars, which would be recorded, on topics ranging from content planning, SEO best practices, social media engagement, and measurement.

A library of resources specific to SEO, social media, and content marketing, in addition to region-specific content, can be centrally maintained at headquarters. At the local level, informal meetings (e.g., brown-bag training sessions) can be conducted with each business unit's content producers to create awareness and communicate the role of optimized and socialized content in the context of the broader business objective. Tactical instruction on keyword usage with SEO copywriting, social promotion of that content, and how to use measurement tools to track contribution and progress can be provided for departmental content producers within each business. As the training initiatives gain traction, Giant Software can establish an internal training and certification program for SEO basics and social networking, with individual, departmental, and business unit level scorecards.

### Process

The importance of processes to scalable SEO, social media, and content marketing within a large organization cannot be overstated. Process can be as straightforward as incorporating SEO best practices into brand identity guidelines or formulating a social media policy that sets standards and expectations for employees.

Companies like Giant Manufacturing can evolve the best-practices insight from outside evaluations into internal guides for extending processes across departments, businesses, and regions. From an "optimize and socialize" content marketing perspective, here are eight key areas for large companies to consider when it comes to identifying processes:

1. *Customer segments and personas.* The continuity of approach for researching customer segments and developing profiles or customer personas will provide more reliable information from which nearly all other content marketing activities will extend. Data collection, evaluation, and clustering to arrive at an archetype for best (and worst) groups of customers can be instrumental for more effective content marketing.

2. *Editorial plan and calendar.* Templates for editorial plans are essential for managing content assets, a schedule of publishing, their relationship with other content, planned repurposing, promotion, and how content is mapped to the appropriate stage in the buying cycle. The process of developing and following the editorial plan will ensure quality and consistency of relevant content to attract, engage, and inspire your customers.

3. *Search keywords and social topics.* Keyword research processes include the creation and maintenance of keyword glossaries that organize and prioritize lists of phrases that can drive relevant search traffic. They also include the use of keyword glossaries by content creation staff for conception, titling, linking, and copywriting. Keywords facilitate content on a variety of publishing platforms, from the corporate website to social content. Making keyword guidance a part of brand identity guidelines can help ensure that high-value phrases are used where it matters most.

4. *Content publishing.* A process for publishing content on a corporate website will involve processes of review and editorial approval that are very different than those followed for social media content such as tweets or Facebook Fan Page updates. Whether content is a video being published to YouTube or a PowerPoint presentation being uploaded to SlideShare, a process will ensure brand, editorial, SEO, and social guidelines are followed.

5. *Content promotion.* Guidelines for content promotion can provide boundaries and best practices for the types of sites and social channels intended for exposure. The editorial plan will indicate specific promotion channels for each type of planned content.

6. *Cross-promotion and integration with other marketing and PR initiatives.* Integration of optimized content with other departmental content can provide new linking opportunities as well as a channel

for exposure to a broader audience. Linking best practices will provide more intentional and targeted anchor text between press releases and product pages or between social status updates and blog posts, facilitating both user and search engine discovery.

7. *Measurement of KPIs and business outcomes.* Following a process for measuring content marketing and optimization performance and business outcomes is essential for a successful program. There are myriad data points that can be reported on with social media monitoring, web analytics, and media tracking. When goals, target audience, planned content, optimization, and promotion are congruent with success measurement, more actionable insights will result.

8. *Reporting segmentation for content producers, marketing, product leadership, and management team.* The value derived from analytics reporting is related to the segmentation of meaningful data to its intended audience. Feedback for content producers will be very different than overall program performance data and trends provided to the business management team. Guidelines for producing relevant and useful reports will ensure their review and ability to inspire action to improve performance.

Each of these areas contains subordinate sequences of tasks, and documenting processes will ensure continuity and quality of content optimization and social promotion relevant to target customer segments for each department, business, and region.

## ASSESSING SEARCH AND SOCIAL MEDIA READINESS AND TRAINING OPPORTUNITIES

Content development occurs across an organization, and your newfound search and social media smarts will be difficult to scale unless you can extend that knowledge to others who are in a position to create and promote content online. No matter what your staff tells you, they will never know enough. There is no end to search and social media expertise for content marketing. The healthiest perspective toward best-practices search and social media optimization with a content marketing strategy is a cycle of planning, deployment, evaluation, and improvement. It's a journey, not a destination. The trick isn't just to identify training opportunities but to plan for ongoing SEO copywriting, content mapping for personas, social media listening, and engagement training for all appropriate

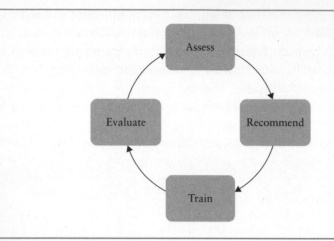

**FIGURE 14.1    The Training Process**

staff on an ongoing basis. I've never run into a company, from start-up to Fortune 50, that didn't need help in those areas. The trick is to identify areas of opportunity and then prioritize. (See Figure 14.1.)

## CONCLUSION

The scale of integrated optimization, social media, and content marketing depends on a combination of people, process, and technology. I hope you see how the puzzle pieces fit together. Applying best practices to processes and training is an integral part of scaling an integrated SEO, social media, and content marketing program. On the companion website, at OptimizeBook.com, I'll be posting videos, reports, and how-to articles covering many of the key principles mentioned in this book, which you can use as a resource in your journey toward an optimized state of mind.

## ACTION ITEMS

1. Take inventory of the processes you currently have in place regarding social media marketing, search engine optimization, and content marketing. Reconcile those processes with any gaps you have identified by reading this book.

2. Pick three tools that would help you make your optimization and social engagement efforts more efficient and scalable.

3. Identify individuals who are in a position to affect the implementation of search, social media, and content marketing initiatives within your company.

4. Identify the key roles and responsibilities those individuals should master.

5. Create an assessment of those skills against the ideal.

6. Develop a training program to get key individuals and the organization up to speed in their ability to plan, create, optimize, promote, and measure content marketing.

# CHAPTER 15

## Are You Optimized?

As online marketers, we're never really fully "optimized." I cannot over-emphasize the importance of understanding that the task of optimizing our search, social media, and content marketing efforts is a journey, not a destination. As long as the environment within the search and social web continue to evolve, change, and innovate, marketers will analyze and refine their online marketing programs to adapt and become more successful. Five years ago, who would have guessed that tablet devices like the iPad and Kindle would have penetrated the market as they have? Who would have guessed that Google and Facebook would have made the dramatic changes that they have, as the lines between search engine and social network have blurred?

Consumer adoption and use of technology is a moving target, and as online marketers with insight into the importance of consumer experience with content, we must be aware of those changes. Seeing future trends is exactly what we need to do in order to better attract, engage, and inspire customers to take action.

### A DIFFERENT WAY OF THINKING ABOUT OPTIMIZATION

Your journey through this book has taken you from creating a road map and strategy at 30,000 feet to diving deeply into a sea of specific tactics, ranging from persona development to keyword optimization to social networking. The tactics discussed within this book will continue to develop and evolve, so view this information as a baseline for gaining an optimized perspective that you can develop and evolve over the long term.

Through this journey, you've learned to seek out and answer the questions that are most important to what your customers care about and how that translates into an effective content marketing strategy. Although we could have focused on the most popular social networks or trendy SEO tactics, a purely tactical approach would not help you develop a sustainable long-term plan for engaging customers and inspiring them to take action. The important homework in understanding customer segments, their goals, and how that translates to optimized and socialized content is an Optimize advantage.

The principles we've covered in *Optimize* show how the thinking about optimization has evolved as it relates to search, social media, and content. For companies that want to survive and thrive on the search and social web, it's an essential change of perspective. If companies would make more of an effort to focus on customer behaviors and preferences for information discovery, user experience, and engagement, it would be a giant step forward in terms of a sustainable content marketing strategy. Something as simple and straightforward as researching the appropriate types of media, topics, and channels preferred by both customers and those who influence customers would offer your company a distinct competitive advantage over what most companies are doing with their online marketing. The good news is that by following the steps and insights in this book, you're already on your way.

## AN "OPTIMIZE AND SOCIALIZE" STATE OF MIND

In this book, we've discussed a three-part optimization approach: (1) how people find information, (2) which formats and topics resonate, and (3) how to inspire interaction, sharing, and commerce. Platforms, applications (apps), and social technologies might change, but a more holistic view of optimization will guide content marketing efforts regardless of which social media, network, or search engine platform rule the day.

The holistic approach to content marketing optimization outlined in this book is in alignment with the actual definition of the word *optimize*: "To make as perfect, effective, or functional as possible." With an "optimize and socialize" approach to content marketing, you can connect your customers with brand content and experiences in a way that motivates them to act: that is, to buy, refer, and/or share. This approach extends beyond a typical buying cycle. Each touch point in the brand and consumer experience across the customer life cycle can be optimized for better performance, whether for referrals, repeat purchases, advocacy, or service.

An optimized state of mind isn't just about how you can sell more products and services to people right now, but rather how you can influence purchases next month, next year, or even five or ten years from now. The concept of discovery, consume, and share is so important because it transcends ideas like "social network" or "search engine" and focuses more on consumers and technologies, whatever they may be. Will we be using a search engine like Google in five years? Will we be using desktop computers in five years? What will future social networks look like? Answers to those questions are answers to the future of online marketing and customer engagement.

## ADAPT OR DIE: COLLECTIVE SOCIAL WISDOM FOR THE WIN

Google, Facebook, Apple, Amazon, and plenty of other large companies are innovating at amazing speed to gain control of consumer and brand attention online. Some are doing it through devices, some through content, others through infrastructure. These few companies have had a huge impact on what we do online; at the same time, new start-ups, like Pinterest and Instagram, are creating amazing solutions. What are you doing to understand the bigger picture and what it means for your business? How are you structuring your business marketing, communications, and use of technology to anticipate and innovate?

Rather than jumping sequentially from one thing to the next, online marketers can develop adaptive models that allow for rapid assimilation of new technologies and trends. Some companies will adopt new social technologies and platforms early and risk failure; others will go with the crowd; and yet others will wait until it's too painful not to change. The ramp-up time to evaluate and adopt new technologies and trends is expensive. For example, more than $100 billion has been invested in social business,[1] and that's just a drop in the bucket compared to anticipated costs over the next five years, as companies implement enterprise collaboration platforms and social technologies.

In order to survive and thrive, more companies are going to hone their ability to adapt more quickly, tune in to trends and data more efficiently, and at the same time develop the infrastructure and partnerships that will allow them to evolve and innovate at greater speed.

On a practical level, the new Internet no longer exists solely on your computer, as both consumers and content shift to tablet devices and smartphones. The search experience has become distinctly different for consumers through innovations such as Google+ integrating with Google search. At the same time, these changes are new opportunities for marketers trying to play Google's game of achieving top search visibility.

Creating an adaptive approach to incorporating new social and web applications, tools, and platforms can filter down the most relevant shiny new objects and allow for more rapid incorporation with content marketing efforts. This approach means coordinating people within your company who can fulfill these roles. For that, some social business and internal collaboration tools will be involved. Leveraging your collective organization to monitor and filter for emerging social technologies relevant to engaging with your customer base can result in more rapid identification, best-practices formulation, and successful implementation. Essentially, a social business is an optimized business. (See Figure 15.1.)

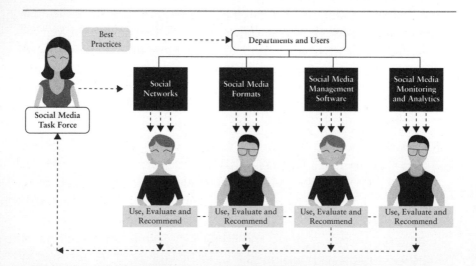

**FIGURE 15.1 Internal Social Collaboration for Monitoring, Testing, and Adopting New Marketing Technology**

Most companies don't have staff or resources dedicated to testing out new social technologies, so why not tap into the collective knowledge, wisdom, and reach of your employees, partners, and even customers? Without the ability to adapt, the momentum of many online marketing efforts will certainly die—or at least lose out to competitors who are paying attention.

An adaptable approach to content and optimized online marketing is about the journey. It's about trying to perfect your craft and continuously refine what you have to work with every day. When you use SEO, social media, and content marketing tools, understand and even anticipate that they will change. Tools are important, but it's also important to focus on whatever it takes to stay connected with your customers and community using the search and social channels that are most relevant.

Imagine how many more changes there will be in technology—and in consumer behaviors—in the coming years. What can you do to prepare for an adaptable online marketing approach? Time will tell when it comes to changes in technology, but when you approach your content marketing strategy with an integrated perspective, there's no telling what results you'll achieve, in both the short and the long term.

## SO, ARE YOU OPTIMIZED?

If your first thought about content and marketing is: "How can I meet the needs of my target audience with content that they care about?" you will be well on your way.

# About the Author

Lee Odden is an internationally known authority on the intersection of Search, Social Media, and Content for marketing and public relations. He serves as the CEO of TopRank Online Marketing, a provider of Internet marketing consulting services for progressive companies in North America and Western Europe. His online marketing consulting experience ranges from helping small businesses get started with social media to consulting with several Fortune 50 companies on SEO.

Odden has been recognized for his expertise with enterprise social media, SEO, and content marketing strategies by *The Economist, Advertising Age,* and Mashable. He writes a monthly column called "Social Media Smarts" for ClickZ, and his blog at TopRankBlog.com has an active community with nearly 50,000 subscribers. TopRank's blog has been rated the number one Content Marketing blog three times by Junta42 and is ranked as a top marketing the blog on the *AdAge* Power 150. Odden has served on the board of advisers for Incisive Media's SES Conference, DMA Search and Social Media Marketing Councils, Minnesota Interactive Marketing Association, and MarketingProfs B2B Forum.

As a popular speaker, Odden has given keynote presentations at numerous conferences, speaks at private corporate events and has been an active participant at search, social media and public relations events around the world.

# Notes

## PHASE 1: PLANNING

### Chapter 1    Setting the Stage for an Optimized State of Mind

1. Kristen Purcell, "Search and email still top the list of most popular online activities," Pew Internet, August 9, 2011, http://www.pewinternet.org/~/media/files/reports/2011/pip_search-and-email.pdf.
2. "comScore Releases September 2011 U.S. Search Engine Rankings," comScore, October 11, 2011, http://www.comscore.com/Press_Events/Press_Releases/2011/10/comScore_Releases_September_2011_U.S._Search_Engine_Rankings.
3. *Twitter,* accessed October 2011, http://twitter.com.
4. *Facebook,* accessed October 2011, facebook.com.
5. Paul Allen, "Google+ reaches 50 Million User Mark in About 88 Days," *Google+,* September 26, 2011, https://plus.google.com/117388252776312694644/posts/EwpnUp TkJ5W.
6. Mary Madden and Kathryn Zickuhr, "65% of online adults use social networking sites," Pew Internet, August 26, 2011, http://pewinternet.org/~/media/Files/Reports/2011/PIP-SNS-Update-2011.pdf.

7. *Google* (blog), accessed 2007, http://googleblog.blogspot.com/.

8. Lee Odden, "SEO 2.- Digital Asset Optimization," *TopRank* (blog), June 14, 2007, http://www.toprankblog.com/2007/06/digital-asset-optimization/.

9. Under The Hood, *Google*, accessed 2011, http://www.google.com/insidesearch/underthe hood.html.

## Chapter 2   Journey: Where Does Optimize and Socialize Fit in Your Company?

1. David Kirkpatrick, "Marketing Strategy: Revenue-oriented approach leads to 700% two-year growth," Marketing Sherpa, June 1, 2011, http://www.marketingsherpa.com/article .php?ident=31928.

2. Lee Odden, "OMS10 B2B Marketing Case Study: Marketo," *TopRank* (blog), February 2010, http://www.toprankblog.com/2010/02/b2b-marketing-case-study-marketo/.

3. "Ernst & Young Previews New Campus Recruitment and Social Media Strategies," PR Newswire, September 23, 2011, http://www.prnewswire.com/news-releases/ ernst—young-previews-new-campus-recruitment-and-social-media-strategies-103640319.html.

## Chapter 3   Smart Marketing Requires Intelligence: Research, Audit, and Listen

1. "Search and Social Together Aid Online Shoppers," *eMarketer,* March 16, 2011, http:// www.emarketer.com/(S(qolko3450oim0q55s152wx45))/Article.aspx?R=1008282.

2. Lee Odden, "Social Media Monitoring - Top 10 Reasons for Monitoring Brands," *TopRank* (blog), May 2011, http://www.toprankblog.com/2008/05/top-10-reasons-for-monitoring-brands-in-social-media/.

3. Lionel Menchaca, "Dell's Next Step: The Social Media Listening Command Center," Dell, December 8, 2010, http://en.community.dell.com/dell-blogs/direct2dell/b/direct 2dell/archive/2010/12/08/dell-s-next-step-the-social-media-listening-command-center .aspx.

4. Adam Ostrow, "Inside Gatorade's Social Media Command Center," *Mashable,* June 15, 2010, http://mashable.com/2010/06/15/gatorade-social-media-mission-control/.

5. Webmaster Central, *Google,* accessed November 2011, http://www.google.com/ webmasters/.

6. Inside Search, *Google,* accessed November 2011, http://www.google.com/insidesearch/ underthehood.html.

7. Webmaster Central, *Google,* accessed December 2011, http://www.google.com/ webmasters/.

8. Webmaster, *Bing,* accessed December 2011, http://www.bing.com/toolbox/webmaster.

## Chapter 4   In It to Win It: Setting Objectives

1. Joe Pulizzi, "What is Content Marketing?" Content Marketing Institute, accessed December 2011, http://www.junta42.com/resources/what-is-content-marketing.aspx.

2. Aho Williamson, "Marketers Spending More on Social Media for the Wrong Reasons," eMarketer, December 27, 2010, http://www.emarketer.com/blog/index.php/marketers-spending-social-media-wrong-reasons/.

3. Michael Brito, "The Book," *Smart Business, Social Business,* accessed December 2011, http://thesocialbusinessbook.com/the-book/.

4. Jeanne Meister and Kate Willyerd, "Intel's Social Media Training," Harvard Business Review, February 3, 2010, http://blogs.hbr.org/cs/2010/02/intels_social_media_employee_t.html.

5. Robin Wauters, "Best Buy Goes All Twitter Crazy With @Twelpforce," *TechCrunch,* July 21, 2009, http://techcrunch.com/2009/07/21/best-buy-goes-all-twitter-crazy-with-twelpforce/.

6. Drew Neisser, "Move Over Social Media; Here Comes Social Business," *Fast Company* (blog), September 11, 2011, http://www.fastcompany.com/1779375/move-over-social-media-here-comes-social-business.

7. Jack Neff, "Sleeping Giant at Walmart Wakes—Its Vast Workforce," *Advertising Age,* November 28, 2011, http://adage.com/article/news/walmart-motivating-mobilizing-workforce/231210/.

8. "Social Media Tools, Online Search Key for Business Journalists According to Survey By BtoB PR Tech Firm Arketi," Arketi Group, June 15, 2009, accessed December 2011, http://www.pitchengine.com/arketigroup/social-media-tools-online-search-key-for-business-journalists-according-to-survey-by-btob-pr-tech-firm-arketi/13743/.

9. "National Survey Finds Majority of Journalists Now Depend on Social Media for Story Research," George Washington University, January 21, 2010, http://www.gwu.edu/explore/mediaroom/newsreleases/nationalsurveyfindsmajorityofjournalistsnow dependonsocialmediaforstoryresearch.

10. Karen O'Leonard, "The Talent Acquisition Factbook 2011," Bersin & Associates, November 2011, http://www.google.com/url?sa=t&rct=j&q=&esrc=s&source=web&cd=2&ved=0CC0QFjAB&url=http%3A%2F%2Ftalent.linkedin.com%2FRegister%2Fdownloadprocess.php%3FID%3D78&ei=BIUET-WUAoKZiQKc0_GzDg&usg=AFQjCNEY3VRkuO2fkN-3qSGhmIZ1ZLn5og.

## Chapter 5  Roadmap to Success: Content Marketing Strategy

1. "comScore Releases November 2011 U.S. Search Engine Rankings," comScore, December 16, 2011, http://www.comscore.com/Press_Events/Press_Releases/2011/12/comScore_Releases_November_2011_U.S._Search_Engine_Rankings.

2. *YouTube,* accessed December 2011, http://www.youtube.com/t/press_statistics.

3. *Facebook,* accessed December 2011, https://www.facebook.com/press/info.php?statistics.

4. "200 million Tweets per day," *Twitter,* June 30, 2011, http://blog.twitter.com/2011/06/200-million-tweets-per-day.html.

5. Jeff Weiner, "100 million members and counting . . ." *LinkedIn* (blog), March 22, 2011, http://blog.linkedin.com/2011/03/22/linkedin-100-million/.

6. "So we grew 3400% last year . . ." *Foursquare* (blog), January 24, 2011, http://blog.foursquare.com/2011/01/24/2010infographic/.

7. Josh Constine, "Pinterest Hits 10 Million U.S. Monthly Uniques Faster Than Any Standalone Site Ever -comScore," *TechCrunch,* February 7, 2012, http://techcrunch.com/2012/02/07/pinterest-monthly-uniques/.

## PHASE 2:    IMPLEMENTATION

### Chapter 6    Know Thy Customer: Personas

1. Adele Revella, "Buyer Persona Manifesto," June 2011, http://www.buyerpersona.com/wp-content/uploads/2011/06/The_Buyer_Persona_Manifesto.pdf.

### Chapter 7    Words Are Key to Customers: Keyword Research

1. Hitwise, "Experian Hitwise reports Google share of searches at 66 percent in July 2011," Experian Hitwise, August 11, 2011, http://www.hitwise.com/us/about-us/press-center/press-releases/experian-hitwise-reports-google-share-of-searche/.
2. "Drive Innovation," *Think Insights with Google,* accessed December 2011, http://www.thinkwithgoogle.com/insights/facts/marketing-objective/.

### Chapter 8    Attract, Engage, and Inspire: Building Your Content Plan

1. Joe Pulizzi, "2012 B2B Content Marketing Benchmarks, Budgets and Trends [Research Report]," December 5, 2011, Content Marketing Institute, http://www.contentmarketing institute.com/2011/12/2012-b2b-content-marketing-research/.
2. MECLABS, "MarketingSherpa's 2012 Search Marketing Benchmark Report SEO Edition," MECLABS, accessed December 2011, http://www.meclabs.com/training/publications/benchmark-report/2012-search-marketing-seo-edition?8907.

### Chapter 9    Content Isn't King, It's the Kingdom: Creation and Curation

1. Mg Siegler, "Eric Schmidt: Every 2 Days We Create As Much Information As We Did Up To 2003," *TechCrunch,* August 4, 2010, http://techcrunch.com/2010/08/04/schmidt-data/.
2. "AOL Research: Content Is The Fuel Of The Social Web," *AOL,* April 28, 2011, http://corp.aol.com/2011/04/28/aol-research-content-is-the-fuel-of-the-social-web/.

### Chapter 10    If It Can Be Searched, It Can be Optimized: Content Optimization

1. Joe Pulizzi, "Content Marketing Playbook 2011 - 42 Ways to Connect with Customers [free eBook]," Content Marketing Institute, August 10, 2011, http://www.contentmarketing institute.com/2011/08/content-marketing-playbook/.

### Chapter 11    Community Rules: Social Network Development

1. Barb Dybwad, "The State of Online Word of Mouth Marketing [STATS]," April 25, 2010, *Mashable,* http://mashable.com/2010/04/25/word-of-mouth-marketing-stats/.
2. "Why do Affluent Consumers Connect with Brands on Social Networks?" eMarketer, May 10, 2011, http://www.public.site2.mirror2.phi.emarketer.com/Article.aspx?R=1008379.

3. "Social Signals Increasingly Important to SEO," *MarketingCharts,* January 9, 2012, http://www.marketingcharts.com/direct/social-signals-increasingly-important-to-seo-20695/.

4. *Facebook,* accessed January 2012, https://www.facebook.com/press/info.php?statistics.

5. Leslie Horn, "Infographic: What Happens Online in 60 Seconds?" *PCMag.com,* December 27, 2011, http://www.pcmag.com/rticle2/0,2817,2398097,00.asp.

6. "Growth of Facebook.com Across Global Regions," comScore Data Mine, May 11, 2011, http://www.comscoredatamine.com/2011/05/growth-of-facebook-com-across-global-regions/.

7. *Check Facebook,* accessed December 2011, http://www.checkfacebook.com/

8. "Frequently Asked Questions," *YouTube,* accessed January 2012, http://www.youtube.com/t/faq.

9. "YouTube," *Wikipedia,* accessed January 2012, http://en.wikipedia.org/wiki/YouTube.

10. "comScore Releases October 2009 U.S. Search Engine Rankings," comScore, November 17, 2009, http://www.comscore.com/Press_Events/Press_Releases/2009/11/comScore_Releases_October_2009_U.S._Search_Engine_Rankings.

11. "YouTube serves up 100 million videos a day online," *USA Today,* July 16, 2006, http://www.usatoday.com/tech/news/2006-07-16-youtube-views_x.htm.

12. Jake Hird, "20+ Mine-blowing social media statistics: One year later," Econsultancy, March 25, 2011, http://econsultancy.com/us/blog/7334-social-media-statistics-one-year-later.

13. "Reaching Your Audience on YouTube," *YouTube,* accessed December 2011, http://www.youtube.com/advertise/demographics.html.

14. "Statistics," *YouTube,* accessed December 2011, http://www.youtube.com/t/press_statistics.

15. *YouTube,* accessed December 2011, http://www.youtube.com/t/press_statistics.

16. EvianBabies, "Evian Roller Babies International Version," *YouTube,* July 1, 2009, http://www.youtube.com/watch?v=XQcVllWpwGs.

17. ciscovid, "The Future of Shopping," *YouTube,* October 2, 2009, http://www.youtube.com/watch?feature=player_embedded&v=jDi0FNcaock

18. *Twitter,* accessed December 2011, http://www.twitter.com.

19. Catherine Smith, "Twitter User Statistics Show Stunning Growth," *Huffington Post,* March 14, 2011, http://www.huffingtonpost.com/2011/03/14/twitter-user-statistics_n_835581.html.

20. *Twitter,* accessed December 2011, http://www.twitter.com.

21. *Twitter,* accessed December 2011, http://www.twitter.com.

22. Stephanie Buck, "A Visual History of Twitter [INFOGRAPHIC]," *Mashable,* September 30, 2011, http://mashable.com/2011/09/30/twitter-history-infographic/.

23. *Hashtracking,* accessed January 2012, http://beta.hashtracking.com/ht-pro-rpt/mackcollier-blogchat-2011-10-30/#tweets.

24. "How LinkedIn Broke Through," Bloomberg *Business Week,* April 10, 2006, http://www.businessweek.com/technology/content/apr2006/tc20060410_185842.htm.

25. LinkedIn Press Center, accessed December 2011, http://press.linkedin.com/about.

26. LinkedIn Press Center, accessed December 2011, http://press.linkedin.com/about.

27. Kipp Bodnar, "Websites Using Google's +1 Button Get 3.5x the Google+ Visits [Data]," *HubSpot* (blog), August 11, 2011, http://blog.hubspot.com/blog/tabid/6307/bid/22293/Websites-Using-Google-s-1-Button-Get-3-5x-the-Google-Visits-Data.aspx.

28. Paul Allen, "Google+ Growth Accelerating, Passes 62 million users. Adding 625,000 new users per day. Prediction: 400 million users by end of 2012," *Google+*, December 27, 2011, https://plus.google.com/117388252776312694644/posts/ZcPA5ztMZaj.

29. Lauren Indvik, "The Top 10 Brand Pages on Google+," *Mashable*, December 21, 2011, http://mashable.com/2011/12/21/top-10-brand-pages-on-google-plus/.

30. Josh Bernoff, "Interactive marketing to exceed ¼ of all ad spend by 2016 (and how we know)," Forrester Research, Inc., August 25, 2011, http://forrester.typepad.com/groundswell/2011/08/interactive-marketing-to-approach-13-of-all-ad-spend-by-2016-and-how-we-know.html.

### Chapter 12    Electrify Your Content: Promotion and Link Building

1. Official Blog, *Google*, accessed January 2012, http://googleblog.blogspot.com/2012/01/search-plus-your-world.html.

2. "MarketingSherpa's 2012 Search Marketing Benchmark Report SEO Edition," MECLABS, accessed January 2012, http://www.meclabs.com/training/publications/benchmark-report/2012-search-marketing-seo-edition?8907.

3. Danny Sullivan, "What Social Signals Do Google & Bing Really Count?" *Search Engine Land*, December 1, 2012, http://searchengineland.com/what-social-signals-do-google-bing-really-count-55389

### Chapter 13    Progress, Refinement, and Success: Measurement

1. "What Twitter Users Think About the Brands They Follow," eMarketer, November 7, 2011, http://www.emarketer.com/Article.aspx?R=1008675.

2. Jefferson Graham, "Coke is a winner on Facebook, Twitter," *USA Today*, November 8, 2011, http://www.usatoday.com/tech/columnist/talkingtech/story/2011-11-08/coca-cola-social-media/51127040/1.

### PHASE 3: SCALE

### Chapter 15    Are you Optimized?

1. Dion Hinchcliffe, "As collaboration goes social, where will it thrive?" *ZDNet*, February 15, 2011, http://www.zdnet.com/blog/hinchcliffe/as-collaboration-goes-social-where-will-it-thrive/1497.

# Index

# TopRank®
## Online Marketing

Get social with TopRank Online Marketing and connect with us for helpful resources, tips, and online marketing consulting services.

- Book Site: optimizebook.com
- Twitter: www.twitter.com/toprank
- Facebook: tprk.us/ombfb
- Google+: tprk.us/trgplus
- Website: www.toprankmarketing.com
- Blog: www.toprankblog.com